MAXIMIZE
YOUR
POTENTIAL

–

amazonpublishing

THE 99U
BOOK SERIES

—

Manage Your Day-to-Day:
*Build Your Routine, Find Your Focus,
and Sharpen Your Creative Mind*

Maximize Your Potential:
*Grow Your Expertise, Take Bold Risks,
and Build an Incredible Career*

MAXIMIZE YOUR POTENTIAL

Grow Your Expertise, Take Bold Risks, and Build an Incredible Career

—

Edited by Jocelyn K. Glei
Foreword by Scott Belsky

Published by Amazon Publishing
PO Box 400818
Las Vegas, NV 89140

ISBN-13: 9781477800898
ISBN-10: 1477800891

For those who strive

WHAT IS 99U?
—

For too long, the creative world has focused on idea generation at the expense of idea execution. As the legendary inventor Thomas Edison famously said, "Genius is 1 percent inspiration, and 99 percent perspiration." To make great ideas a reality, we must act, experiment, fail, adapt, and learn on a daily basis.

99U is Behance's effort to provide this "missing curriculum" for making ideas happen. Through our Webby Award–winning website, popular events, and bestselling books, we share pragmatic, action-oriented insights from leading researchers and visionary creatives.

At 99U, we don't want to give you more ideas—we want to empower you to make good on the ones you've got.

PREFACE

—

Comedian Milton Berle used to say, "If opportunity doesn't knock, build a door." If we want to realize our full potential as creatives and individuals, being proactive isn't just an option, it's a requirement. Fortunately, we have more power than ever to share our ideas with the world, to connect with others, and to define our career paths. The era of self-invention is upon us.

Where we used to associate a career with a slow rise within a single company, we are now switching jobs eleven times on average in our lifetime. Where we used to rely on dealers to share our artwork with the world, we can now simply build an online gallery to share new work as we produce it. Where we used to turn to a small cadre of investors to approve our ideas for creation, we can now pitch our projects to the masses and crowd-source funding online.

The possibilities are infinite. But so, too, are the responsibilities. Having the ability to chart your own course shifts the onus of leadership back onto you. This means that we cannot expect our managers to take charge of our career development and groom us for greatness. We cannot wait quietly for the perfect mentor to arrive and guide us in the development of our craft. And we cannot count on a future filled with signposts and certainty.

To help guide you through this brave new world, 99U's *Maximize Your Potential* assembles insights around four key areas that we believe are essential to long-term career success: identifying and creating new opportunities, cultivating your expertise over time, building collaborative relationships, and learning how to take risks.

Dedicating a chapter to each of these focus areas, we've assembled an incredible group of creative minds—Bob Safian, Ben Casnocha, Joshua Foer, Teresa Amabile, Tony Schwartz, Tina Seelig, and many more—to share their wisdom with you. Drawing on intensive research and deep personal experience, the essays in *Maximize Your Potential* provide a powerhouse of perspectives on how to build a career filled with excitement, achievement, and meaning.

Let this volume be your guide as you craft—and re-craft—your own creative career over time, constantly striving to up the ante on just who you can become.

— *JOCELYN K. GLEI, editor-in-chief, 99U*

TABLE
OF
CONTENTS

BUILDING EXPERTISE

CULTIVATING RELATIONSHIPS

TAKING RISKS

CODA: A FINAL REFLECTION

YOU'RE A FREE RADICAL, RUN WITH IT

—

by Scott Belsky, Founder of Behance

When it comes to our careers and our experience at work, we've become selfish—but in a good way. Getting paid is no longer enough; we expect to actually learn on the job. We want our skills to be fully utilized and are left unsatisfied by "easy jobs." We want more responsibility when we're ready, rather than waiting until we've "put in our time." We expect to do more of what we love, automating the more laborious and monotonous parts of our work.

We are an ambitious and impatient cohort, and rightly so. Why? Because we've entered a new era that empowers us to unleash our full potential. But opportunity and achievement do not flow from a sense of entitlement. Your ability to realize your potential will depend upon your willingness to hone your skills, to take bold risks, and to put your ego on the line in pursuit of something greater.

Chalk it up to new technology, social media, or the once out-of-reach business tools now at your fingertips. The fact is, we're empowered to work on our own terms and do more with less. As a result, we expect more from those that employ us and we expect more from ourselves. When we get the resources and opportunities we deserve, we create the future. If you're reading this book, I suspect you identify.

Here's a name for us: Free Radicals.

Free Radicals want to take their careers into their own hands and put the world to work for them. Free Radicals are resilient, self-reliant, and extremely potent. You'll find them working solo, in small teams, or within large companies. As the world changes, Free Radicals have re-imagined "work" as we know it. No doubt, we have lofty expectations.

We do work that is, first and foremost, intrinsically rewarding. But, we don't create solely for ourselves, we want to make a real and lasting impact in the world around us.

We thrive on flexibility and are most productive when we feel fully engaged. We demand freedom, whether we work within companies or on our own, to run experiments, participate in multiple projects at once, and move our ideas forward.

We make stuff often, and therefore, we fail often. Ultimately, we strive for little failures that help us course-correct along the way, and we view every failure as a learning opportunity, part of our experiential education.

We have little tolerance for the friction of bureaucracy, old-boy networks, and antiquated business practices. As often as possible, we question "standard operating procedure" and assert ourselves. But even when we can't, we don't surrender to the friction of the status quo. Instead, we find clever ways (and hacks) around it.

We expect to be fully utilized and constantly optimized, regardless of whether we're working in a start-up or a large organization. When our contributions and learning plateau, we leave. But when we're leveraging a large company's resources to make an impact in something we care about, we are thrilled! We want to always be doing our best work and making the greatest impact we can.

We consider open source technology, APIs, and the vast collective knowledge of the Internet to be our personal arsenal. *Wikipedia*, Quora, and open communities for designers, developers, and thinkers were built by us and for us. Whenever possible, we leverage collective knowledge to help us make better decisions for ourselves and our clients. We also contribute to these open resources with a "pay it forward" mentality.

We believe that "networking" is sharing. People listen to (and follow) us because of our discernment and curatorial instinct. As we share our creations as well as what fascinates us, we authentically build a community of supporters who give us feedback, encouragement, and lead us to new opportunities. For this reason and more, we often (though, not always) opt for transparency over privacy.

We believe in meritocracy and the power of online networks and peer communities to advance our ability to do what we love, and do well by doing it. We view competition as a positive motivator rather than a threat, because we want the best idea—and the best execution—to triumph.

We make a great living doing what we love. We consider ourselves to be both artisans and businesses. In many cases, we are our own accounting department, Madison Avenue marketing agency, business development manager, negotiator, and salesperson. We spend the necessary energy to invest in ourselves as businesses—leveraging the best tools and knowledge (most of which are free and online) to run ourselves as a modern-day enterprise.

99U was founded with the Free Radical in mind, to provide education and insights that we didn't get in school but sorely need as we mine opportunities in this new era of work. The book ahead is all about maximizing your potential and taking the reins on your career. I encourage you to absorb these insights, remembering that you're in charge now. With the wind at your back, the responsibility is now yours: challenge and improve yourself—and the world—in every way you can.

CHAPTER ONE

CREATING

OPPORTUNITIES

–

*How to identify and capitalize
on new career opportunities*

Traditional career advice suggests a passive approach to finding your calling: Pick a job listing, apply, wait for a response. Get the job, perform your duties, wait for a promotion. Rinse, repeat, stagnate. But a wait-and-see attitude is hardly the path to greatness.

With the access and resources of the twenty-first century at our fingertips, we can and should be active participants in shaping our future. We must seek out opportunity by strategizing with the resourcefulness and adaptability of a start-up entrepreneur, and we must draw opportunity to us by relentlessly developing our raw skills—excelling at our craft in a way that cannot go unnoticed.

We must look at the market and align our interests and abilities with something that people actually want. And we must keep an ear to the ground for the unexpected—never holding so tightly to our plans that we let luck pass us by.

Greatness doesn't come from taking a "lean back" approach to career planning. Get out in front of opportunity—and it will come to you.

CULTIVATING YOUR CRAFT BEFORE YOUR PASSION

—

Cal Newport

"Follow your passion" is bad advice. I reached this conclusion after spending a year researching a basic question: What makes people love what they do for a living? This research turned up two strikes against the idea of following passion. First, it turns out that few people have pre-existing passions that they can match to a job. Telling them to "follow their passion," therefore, is a recipe for anxiety and failure.

Second, even when people do feel strongly about a particular topic, decades of research on career satisfaction teaches us that you need much more than a pre-existing interest to transform your work into something you love. Many a passionate baker, for example, crumbled under the stress of trying to run a retail bakery, just as many a passionate amateur photographer has lost interest in the art when forced to document yet another interminable wedding.

If you want to end up passionate about your working life, therefore, you need a strategy that's more sophisticated than simply trying to discover some innate calling hardwired in your DNA. In this piece, I want to explore one such strategy—one that turned up often when I studied the lives of people who have built compelling careers. Let's take a well-known literary personality as our case study.

Bill McKibben is an environmental journalist. He became famous for his 1989 book, *The End of Nature*, which was one of the first popular accounts of climate change. He has since written more than a dozen books and become a prominent environmental activist. If you attend a McKibben talk or read a McKibben interview, you'll encounter someone who is obviously passionate about his work. But how did he get to where he is today?

We can pick up McKibben's story when he arrives at Harvard as an undergraduate and signs up to write for the student newspaper, *The Harvard Crimson*. By the time he graduates, he is the paper's editor. This puts him on the radar of *New Yorker* editor William Shawn, who taps the recent grad to write for Talk of the Town, a column that runs at the front of the magazine.

In 1987, five years after arriving at the *New Yorker*, McKibben makes his move. He quits the magazine and moves to a cabin in the

Adirondacks. Sequestered in the wilderness, McKibben pens *The End of Nature*, which becomes an instant classic in environmental journalism, laying the foundation for the passionate life that he enjoys today.

McKibben's story highlights two lessons that my research has shown to be crucial for understanding how people build working lives they love.

LESSON 1:
WHAT YOU DO FOR A LIVING MATTERS LESS THAN YOU THINK

McKibben built a career he loved as a writer. Having studied him, however, I would argue that there are many different career paths he could have followed with an equal degree of passion. The two things that seem to really matter to McKibben are autonomy (e.g., control over what he works on, when he works on it, where he lives, etc.) and having an impact on the world. Therefore, any job that could provide him autonomy and impact would generate passion. One could imagine, for example, an alternative universe in which we find an equally happy McKibben at the head of, say, an important education non-profit or as a respected sociology professor.

This pattern is common in people who love what they do. Their satisfaction doesn't come from the details of their work but instead from a set of important lifestyle traits they've gained in their career. These desirable traits differ for different people—some might crave respect and importance, for example, while others crave flexibility in their schedule and simplicity—but the key point here is that these traits are more general than any specific position. To build a career, the right question is not "What job am I passionate about doing?" but instead "What way of working and living will nurture my passion?"

LESSON 2: SKILL PRECEDES PASSION

McKibben was able to gain autonomy and impact in his career only after he became really good at writing. When he first arrived at Harvard, for example, he was not a great journalist. His early articles, which can be found in the *Crimson* archive, show a beginner's tendency toward overwriting—a 1979 report on the opening game of the Celtics basketball season, for example, describes the arena as an "age-crusted catacomb" and references the team's retired uniform numbers as "a list of saints, identified only by the Kelly-green number that they once wore, dangling from the skylights."

What McKibben's colleagues remember most about him was not some innate gift for his craft but rather his tenacity in working to improve it. Part of *Crimson* lore is the night when McKibben returned to the office late after a Cambridge city council meeting. There were only thirty-five minutes until the next day's articles needed to be finalized. He bet his fellow writers a bottle of Scotch that he could finish three stories before the deadline. He won that bottle.

All told, McKibben wrote more than four hundred articles as a college reporter. He next spent five years writing for the *New Yorker*, which publishes forty-seven issues a year. By the time he made his pivot toward a life of autonomy and impact—moving to the mountains to write *The End of Nature*—he had developed a tremendous amount of professional skill to support this transition. If he had tried to become a full-time book writer earlier in his career, he almost certainly would have failed.

This pattern is common in the lives of people who end up loving their work. As described in Lesson 1, careers become compelling once they feature the general traits you seek. These traits, however, are rare and valuable—no one will hand you a lot of autonomy or impact just because you really want it, for example. Basic economics tells us that if you want something rare and valuable, you need to offer something rare and valuable in return—and in the working world, what you have to offer are your skills. This is why the systematic development of skill (such as McKibben ripping through more than five hundred articles between 1979 and 1987) almost always precedes passion.

Now let's step back and pull the pieces together. The goal of feeling passionate about your work is sound. But following your passion—choosing a career path solely because you are already passionate about the nature of the work—is a poor strategy for accomplishing this goal. It assumes that you have a pre-existing passion to follow that matches up to a viable career, and that matching your work to a strong interest is sufficient to build long-term career satisfaction. Both of these assumptions are flawed.

Bill McKibben's story, by contrast, highlights a more sophisticated strategy for cultivating passion—one deployed by many who end up with compelling careers. It teaches us that we should begin by systematically developing rare and valuable skills. Once we've caught the attention of the marketplace, we can then use these skills as leverage to direct our career toward the general lifestyle traits (autonomy, flexibility, impact, growth, etc.) that resonate with us.

This strategy is less sexy than the idea that choosing the perfect job can provide you with instant and perpetual occupational bliss. But it has the distinct advantage that it actually works.

Put another way: don't follow your passion, cultivate it.

CAL NEWPORT is a writer and a professor at Georgetown University. His book So Good They Can't Ignore You *argues that "follow your passion" is bad advice. Find out more about Cal and his writing at his blog,* Study Hacks.

→ calnewport.com/blog

"The artist is nothing without the gift,

but the gift is nothing without the work."

— ÉMILE ZOLA

REDISCOVERING YOUR ENTREPRENEURIAL INSTINCT

—

Ben Casnocha

Muhammad Yunus, Nobel Peace Prize winner and microfinance pioneer, says, "All human beings are entrepreneurs. When we were in the caves, we were all self-employed . . . finding our food, feeding ourselves. That's where human history began. As civilization came, we suppressed it. We became 'labor' because they stamped us, 'You are labor.' We forgot that we are entrepreneurs."

All humans are entrepreneurs not because all people should start companies, but because the will to create and forage and adapt is part of our DNA. As Yunus says, these qualities are the essence of entrepreneurship. To adapt to the challenges of the world today, you need to rediscover these entrepreneurial instincts.

One of the best ways to do this is to think of yourself as an entrepreneur at the helm of a living, growing start-up venture: *your career*. When you start a company, you make decisions in an information-poor, time-compressed, resource-constrained environment. There are no guarantees or safety nets; dealing with risk is inevitable. The competition is changing and the market is changing. These realities—the ones entrepreneurs face when starting and growing companies—are ones we *all* now face when fashioning a career in any industry. Information is limited. Resources are tight. Competition is fierce.

Becoming the CEO of your career isn't easy; it requires a particular mind-set and a specific set of skills.

KEEPING YOURSELF IN PERMANENT BETA

Technology companies often keep the "beta" label on software for a time after the official launch to stress that the product is not finished so much as ready for the next batch of improvements. Gmail, for example, launched in 2004 but only left official beta in 2009, after millions of people were already using it. Jeff Bezos, founder and CEO of Amazon, concludes every annual letter to shareholders by reminding readers, as he did in his first letter in 1997, that "it's still Day 1" at Amazon.com: "Though we are optimistic, we must remain vigilant and maintain a sense of urgency." In other words, Amazon is never finished: It's always Day 1. For entrepreneurs, finished is an f-word.

Finished ought to be an f-word for all of us. We are all works in progress. Each day presents an opportunity to learn more, do more, be more, and grow more. Keeping yourself in "permanent beta" makes you acknowledge that you have bugs, that there's more testing to do on yourself, and that you will continue to adapt and evolve. It means a lifelong commitment to continuous personal growth. It is a mind-set brimming with optimism because it celebrates the fact that you have the power to improve yourself and, more important, improve the world around you.

EMPLOYING YOUR ENTREPRENEURIAL SKILLS

But a different mind-set alone is not enough. Rediscovering your entrepreneurial instincts is not enough. To thrive as a creative, entrepreneurial professional, you have to acquire the skills to adapt to modern challenges. Here are a few specific suggestions:

1. **Focus on building a competitive advantage.** Ask yourself, "In which ways am I better and different from other people who do similar work?" If you stopped going into the office one day, what would not get done? Just as business entrepreneurs focus on how their company can deliver a product faster/better/cheaper than other companies, you should be identifying how your combination of assets (skills, strengths, contacts) and aspirations (dreams, values, interests) can create a unique offering in the career marketplace. Other professionals are competing for the same desirable opportunities—develop the skills or relationships or interests that will make you stand out from others in your industry.

2. **Plan to adapt.** Entrepreneurs are supremely adaptable. Just consider all the companies that pivoted away from their original idea, such as Starbucks, Flickr, PayPal, and Pixar, to name a few. But

entrepreneurs also engage in thoughtful planning. They make *flexible* plans. Each of us must do the same in our career. Set a Plan A that's your current implementation of building a competitive advantage (your current job, hopefully), but also have a Plan B—something you could pivot to that's different from but related to your current work. Finally, have a steady Plan Z—a worst-case scenario plan in which you might move back in with your parents or cash out your 401(k). With a Plan A, Plan B, and Plan Z, you'll be thinking carefully about your future yet also braced for radical change.

3. Build a network of both close allies and looser acquaintances. Entrepreneurs, contrary to stereotype, are not lone heroes; they rely on networks of people around them to grow their company. You need to grow a team around you, too. We hear a lot about networking, but there's a big difference between being the most-connected person and the best-connected person. One just has a long address book. The other has built a balanced set of strong alliances and looser acquaintances. Your allies are the people you review life goals with, the people you trust, the people with whom you try to work proactively on projects. Acquaintances are valuable because they tend to be folks who work in different companies, industries, or cities. They introduce the strength of diversity into your network. Connect in both ways and you'll be ready to tackle challenging projects with plenty of hands-on support while enjoying a fresh stream of ideas and inspiration from people who run in different social and professional circles.

4. Take intelligent risks. Risk tends to get a bad rap. But it's not the enemy. Entrepreneurs proactively yet prudently take on intelligent risk. Because the flip side of every opportunity is risk, if you're not taking risks, you're not finding the breakout opportunities you're looking for. In your career, good entrepreneurial risks include taking on side projects on nights and weekends, embarking on international travel, asking your boss for extra work, and applying for jobs that you don't think you're fully qualified for.

You change, the competition changes, and the world changes. What cannot change is your determination to continue investing in yourself. Steve Jobs once called Apple the "biggest start-up on the planet." In the same way, you need to stay young, agile, and adaptive. You need to forever be a start-up.

The start-up is *you*.

BEN CASNOCHA *is an entrepreneur and author. He is coauthor, with Reid Hoffman, of* The Start-Up of You: Adapt to the Future, Invest in Yourself, and Transform Your Career, *and author of* My Start-Up Life: What a (Very) Young CEO Learned on His Journey Through Silicon Valley. BusinessWeek *named him one of America's best young entrepreneurs.*

→ www.casnocha.com

"The best way to predict the future is to create it."

— PETER DRUCKER

Q&A:

RE-IMAGINING YOUR
CAREER, CONSTANTLY

—

with Robert Safian

As editor of *Fast Company*, Robert Safian lives at the intersection of design, technology, and creativity—monitoring the pulse of new trends in our businesses and our careers. In a 2012 cover story, he coined the term "Generation Flux" to describe those who will survive and thrive in this complex new world of work. Among others, signature GenFlux capabilities include being adept at developing new skills and being naturally at ease with uncertainty—no small feat to be sure. We chatted with Safian about what flux means for the future of creative careers and how we can excel at coping with it.

Do you think that careers in the traditional sense exist anymore?

I think careers have always been mythic. There's this idea that you would get a job somewhere, work your way up the ladder for forty years, and retire with a gold watch. If that myth were ever true, it's certainly not true anymore. The average amount of time that an American worker stays in his or her current job is 4.4 years. That means we're changing jobs all the time, and yet we're still seeking careers that are more steady than that.

What kinds of skills should people be cultivating?

I think the most important skill in the age of flux is the ability to get new skills. To constantly be open to new areas of learning and new areas of growth. That is what will make you most valuable to the employer, partner, start-up of the future. And it is also what gives you the most options moving forward. That doesn't mean that you should be a dilettante. You have to develop a certain level of expertise in whatever area you choose. But you need to have very little tolerance for stagnation, and if something you're working on doesn't go the way you wanted, you need to have a high capacity for discarding it and moving on to something else.

How does that mind-set play out in practice?

It means that when you have an opportunity to learn and interact with something new, you should be running toward it instead of running away from it. If you have a strong passion and you want to go deep in that one place, go deep. But don't be surprised if you end up going deep in the wrong place. And know that, at some point, you'll pull back and start again somewhere else. That's just the way it's going to be in the time of flux.

If you don't have one place where you really have a passion to go deep, then dig into all the areas in which you're interested. For me, in the world of flux, I think there's no single model that's going to work. There's no single model that's going to work for a company, and there's no single model that's going to work for a career. The time we're coming out of, we're trained to be looking for one answer, one way. Here's how I get from here to there. Here is the career track. Here is the ladder. But that one way doesn't exist anymore.

Do you think it's more about having a personal mission that becomes a compass for making decisions in your career?

I think that the guiding principle is your own passion and your own search for meaning. What mission are you on? What is the mission that you are trying to fulfill in your life that gives your business meaning, that gives your work meaning? And the answer to that may change over time. You may have various missions during the course of your life. But that's what will dictate how you should be spending your energy.

In my experience, people who love what they do are much better at it. They're more successful, are constantly adding new skills, and continue to drive themselves forward. The more passion you can find around what you're doing, the more voracious you'll be in adding and building the skills that will be useful for you in the long run.

There's this saying, "The moment you move to protecting the status quo instead of disrupting the status quo, you put yourself at risk." That's the challenge for businesses, and that's the challenge for individuals: understanding the point at which you are protecting what you know and defending what you know, instead of looking at what else you can learn and how you can grow.

ROBERT SAFIAN *oversees the editorial operations of* Fast Company *and its digital affiliates. He was previously executive editor at* Time *and* Fortune, *and led* Money *magazine for six years.*

→ www.fastcompany.com

"The measure of intelligence is the ability to change."

— ALBERT EINSTEIN

MAKING YOUR
OWN LUCK

—

Jocelyn K. Glei

**If the twentieth-century career was a ladder that
we climbed from one predictable rung to the next,
the twenty-first-century career is more like a
broad rock face that we are all free-climbing.
There's no defined route, and we must use our own
ingenuity, training, and strength to rise to the top.
We must make our own luck.**

The lightning-fast evolution of technology means that jobs can
now become indispensable or outmoded in a matter of years, even
months. Who knew what a "community manager" was ten years ago?
What about an "iPad app designer" or a "JavaScript ninja"?

A substantial portion of the working population now earns its livelihood doing jobs that didn't exist ten or twenty years ago. And even if the nature of your job hasn't changed, chances are you're using new and unanticipated technology and skills to perform that job. Think of the designer who blogs, the comedian who tweets, or the filmmaker who raises a budget on Kickstarter.

Ten years from now, we'll probably all be doing some new type of work that we couldn't possibly imagine today. That thought is both exhilarating and frightening. How do we prepare for a future filled with uncertainty?

1. Look beyond the job title, and focus on your mission. It's easy to get sucked into chasing after a specific job title—whether it's becoming a creative director, a chief marketing officer, or a product manager. But titles are a trap. The job you want today may not exist tomorrow. Thus, by tailoring your goals and your skill development to attaining a specific position, you limit your options.

Rather than setting your sights on a specific role, focus instead on what you want to accomplish. Ask yourself: "What problem am I solving? What do I want to create? What do I want to change?" Your mission will spring from the answers. It could look like: "I want to invent a new business model for online publishing," or "I want to use technology to bring education to underserved communities," or "I want to be part of the conversation about clean energy."

By adopting a mission, you reframe your ambitions in a way that allows other people to get excited and connect with you (e.g., "I'm passionate about clean energy, too. Do you know Mosaic, the clean energy investment marketplace?"). It also gives you a better baseline for aligning your values with potential companies and collaborators. Sure, the company you're interviewing with may need a product manager, but do they share your passion for bringing education to underserved communities?

The more clarity you have in your stated mission, the better equipped you'll be to adapt in a changing marketplace and to attract and assess new opportunities.

2. Explore new technologies with enthusiasm. The tools you use today will not be the tools you use in the future. You may have heard the term "life sport" before. It refers to sports—like golf, tennis, or swimming—that you can play from ages seven to seventy. *Wired* co-founder Kevin Kelly recently expanded this concept to include technology as life sport, outlining a list of "techno life skills" that we should all cultivate.

As Kelly puts it: "If you are in school today the technologies you will use as an adult tomorrow have not been invented yet. Therefore, the life skill you need most is not the mastery of specific technologies, but mastery of . . . how technology in general works." [1]

Whether it's interviewing someone over Skype, developing an affable Twitter persona, learning how to publish an e-book, or experimenting with a new task management app, we must become adept at testing out new technologies that can benefit us in our personal and professional lives. Sometimes, we will choose *not* to integrate a new technology into our lives, and that's okay. It's the experimentation, and the awareness we gain through it, that's key.

3. Make a habit of helping people whenever you can. We can all be pretty sure we're going to need help at some point in the future. As leadership expert and ethnographer Simon Sinek articulated in a rousing talk at our 99U Conference, "We're not good at everything; we're not good by ourselves." Sinek went on to describe how the ability to build relationships is the key to our survival as a race *and* to thriving as idea-makers. The number one way to build relationships is, of course, by helping each other.

But in an age of complex connections and contingencies, there isn't always a simple one-to-one correlation among acts of generosity. (As in, "I'll scratch your back, you scratch mine.") And there shouldn't be. Helping our peers, colleagues, and allies should be a regular habit and its own reward. We usually can't foresee how, but the goodness always comes back around.

4. Be proactive about taking on additional responsibilities and pitching new projects. The days of "grooming" young employees for senior positions are over. No one is going to spend more time thinking about your career than you are. (And, honestly, why would you expect them to?) As *New York Times* columnist and bestselling author Thomas Friedman wrote, employers "are all looking for the same kind of people—people who not only have the critical thinking skills to do the value-adding jobs that technology can't but also people who can invent, adapt, and reinvent their jobs every day, in a market that changes faster than ever." [2]

You won't be rewarded with exciting new opportunities by keeping your head down and following the rules. If you want a new challenge at work or more responsibility, it's on you to pitch your boss or your client on what needs to be done, why it's a good idea, why you're the best person to do it, and why everyone will benefit. Lead the way with your own creativity and initiative, and back it up with enthusiasm and a strong business case.

5. Cultivate your "luck quotient" by staying open and alert. A chance meeting at a coffee shop leads you to your first business partner, a friend of a friend introduces you to a mentor who changes your life, a comment you posted on a blog ends up landing you a new writing gig. These are the kinds of chance events we chalk up to luck, as though they are totally out of our control.

But it turns out that, far from being a mysterious force, luck is the outcome of a specific set of character traits. Being lucky is actually a way of being in the world—and it's one that you can cultivate. Here's what Tina Seelig, executive director of the Stanford Technology Ventures Program (whom we'll interview later in this book) wrote in her excellent book *What I Wish I Knew When I Was 20*:

> *Lucky people take advantage of chance occurrences that come their way. Instead of going through life on cruise control, they pay attention to what's happening around them and, therefore, are able to extract greater value from each situation . . . Lucky people are also open to novel opportunities and willing to try things outside of their usual experiences. They're more inclined to pick up a book on an unfamiliar*

> *subject, to travel to less familiar destinations, and
> to interact with people who are different than
> themselves.*[3]

In short, lucky people are open-minded, upbeat, proactive, and always willing to try something new. While it's good to be directed in your career, you'll want to stay open and alert to unexpected possibilities. And when they show up, act on them. You never know what the outcome might be.

6. Always be asking "What's next?" If you're not asking questions, you're not going to find answers. We often wait to ask those hard career questions right up until the moment when we need the answer desperately. We wait until we get laid off to think about what's next. Or we wait until we're completely miserable and burned-out at our current job before we even begin to contemplate the next one.

But if you're going to switch jobs every four years or so, you should be asking yourself "What's next?" all the time. Not in a way that disengages you from your current position, of course, but rather in a way that helps you push yourself and hone in on your passion. What new skills do you want to develop? To whom should you reach out to be your mentor? Should you take on that big new project at work—the one that kind of scares you?

If you don't ask, you'll never find out.

JOCELYN K. GLEI leads the 99U in its mission to provide the "missing curriculum" on making ideas happen. She oversees the Webby Award–winning 99u.com website and curates the popular 99U Conference. Jocelyn is also the editor of the 99U book series, which includes the titles Manage Your Day-to-Day *and this book,* Maximize Your Potential.

→ www.jkglei.com

"Luck is what happens when preparation meets opportunity."

— SENECA

FINDING YOUR WORK SWEET SPOT

—

Scott Belsky

There are two types of work in this world. The first is the obligatory kind, the work we do because of a job or a contract, often with an eye on the clock. The second—very different—type of work we do is "work with intention."

When we are working with intention, we toil away endlessly—often through the wee hours of the morning—on projects we care about deeply. Whether it's building an intricate model of an ancient ship, writing a song, or mapping out an idea for your first business, you do it out of genuine interest and love.

If you can make "work with intention" the center of your efforts, you're more likely to make an impact on what matters most to you. But how do you actually do that?

Over the years, I've met many creative leaders and entrepreneurs who have made an impact in their respective industries. It should come as no surprise that they love what they do. But when I've asked probing questions about their career paths, I always find that their good fortune was anything but predestined. Aside from lots of hard work, great creative careers are powered by an intersection of three factors: interest, skill, and opportunity.

The same thinking applies to successful creative projects. The magic happens when you find the sweet spot where these three factors intersect.

1. YOUR (GENUINE) INTERESTS

What fascinates you? What topic do you like to discuss and read about the most? Many legendary creative careers are sparked by a genuine interest in a particular field. Perhaps it's film, coffee, or airplane travel. This is not about what promises the most economic gain. On the contrary, this is a topic that trumps economic concerns because you love it so much.

While money is important, the drive that powers the most remarkable achievements comes from a deeper place. To understand the symptoms of work performed without genuine interest, look no further than the nearest abandoned project or malnourished career. Look to the middle managers who count down to five o'clock. It's not pretty.

Reaching for greatness without a genuine interest in the field is like running a marathon after fasting. Remarkable achievements are fueled by genuine interest.

2. YOUR KEY SKILLS

What are your skills and your natural gifts? Do you have a knack for math or storytelling? Perhaps you possess a unique understanding of the human condition? Take an inventory of what you know or could easily learn. The skills you have are helpful indicators of the opportunities that are most likely to flourish under your leadership. Of course, skills alone are insufficient. But when paired with a genuine interest and a new opportunity, your innate capabilities can truly shine, opening the path to success.

3. YOUR "OPPORTUNITY STREAM"

The third factor that plays into every successful career is opportunity. Unfortunately, this is often where we get stuck, discounting the potential opportunities that surround us as inadequate. There is no such thing as equal access to opportunity. "Old boy" networks and nepotism run rampant in all industries. And most opportunities are entirely circumstantial. As such, you must simply define "opportunity" as anything that brings you a step closer to your genuine interest.

Opportunity is less about leaps forward and more about slow but steady progress. Most folks I meet can track their greatest opportunities back to chance conversations. This is why personal introductions, conferences, and other networking efforts really pay off. Just surrounding yourself with more activity will inherently increase your "opportunity stream"—the chance happenings that lead you closer to your genuine interests.

WORKING AT THE I.S.O
(INTEREST, SKILLS, OPPORTUNITY) INTERSECTION

When you make choices that will affect your career, aim for the intersection of your genuine interests, skills, and opportunities.

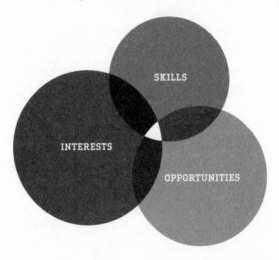

Contemplate the three circles of the Venn diagram above—one circle encompasses your genuine interests; one, your skills; and one, the stream of opportunities available to you. An intersection between just two of the circles doesn't cut it. A love for basketball and a connection to an NBA scout won't help you if you lack the skills to play ball. You need to find your trifecta: the intersection of your interests, skills, and opportunities (ISO).

When you engage with a project in your ISO, you've entered your zone of maximum impact. In such a state, you are a potent force of nature—your avocation becomes your vocation. You can work with full conviction, without ambiguity, and you can transcend your reliance on short-term rewards and societal approval. This is where the magic happens.

As leaders, we must help our partners and employees find work in their ISO. Legendary managers seek to understand the genuine interests and skills of their employees and are constantly trying to create opportunities within those intersections.

Want to change the world? Push everyone you know to work within their ISO. Mentor people to help them realize their genuine interests and skills and capitalize on even the smallest opportunities around them. When it comes to your own career, make every decision with a constant eye toward your own intersection.

A career of "work with intention" is the kind that moves industries forward. Do it for yourself and for the rest of us.

SCOTT BELSKY is Adobe's Vice President of Community and head of Behance, the leading online platform for creatives to showcase and discover creative work. Scott has been called one of the "100 Most Creative People in Business" by Fast Company, and is the author of the international bestseller Making Ideas Happen. *He is also an investor and adviser for several companies, including Pinterest and Uber.*

→ www.scottbelsky.com

KEY
TAKEAWAYS

—

Creating Opportunities

Get more insights and the desktop wallpaper at:

→ www.99u.com/opportunity

CRAFT COMES BEFORE PASSION

Passion isn't a profession, it's a way of working. To achieve a lifestyle (and workstyle) that you love, start by cultivating rare and valuable skills that will set you apart.

PLAN TO ADAPT YOUR PLAN

Plan flexibly, and be ready to pivot in your career if necessary. Always have a Plan A, B, and even Z in your back pocket.

DON'T SETTLE FOR THE STATUS QUO

Try to regularly "disrupt" your own status quo. If you're getting too comfortable in your current position, it's probably time to challenge yourself in new ways.

GET MISSION CRITICAL

Think about your work—and where you are going—in terms of a larger mission. A job title is a closed objective, but a mission can grow with you.

LUCK IS A STATE OF MIND

Expose yourself to new situations, keep an open mind, and be proactive about pursuing chance opportunities. Luck comes to those who seek it.

WORK WITH INTENTION

Calibrate your career for maximum impact by working at the intersection of your genuine skills, interests, and opportunities.

CHAPTER TWO

BUILDING

EXPERTISE

–

*How to build and optimize
your skills over time*

It's easy to sleepwalk through life, to operate at the level of "good enough," to define a destination and then go on autopilot. But if we want to truly excel in our careers, we must awaken to our own profound capacity for growth. Our intelligence, our talents, and even our habits are all remarkably malleable.

This is good news because the market—for skills, for jobs, for big ideas—is changing faster than ever. The areas of expertise that are in demand today won't be the same five years from now. Therefore, the people who can constantly adapt and update their arsenal of talents will have a distinct advantage.

We must adopt a mind-set that fosters constant growth, dedicate ourselves to the regular and rigorous practice of our craft, and track our setbacks and successes over time. We must set the bar high, raise it, and raise it again.

If you want to stand out in this world, stepping out of your comfort zone—and cultivating new skills—is the place to start.

FOCUSING ON GETTING BETTER, RATHER THAN BEING GOOD

—

Heidi Grant Halvorson

People with above-average aptitudes—the ones we recognize as being especially clever, creative, insightful, or otherwise accomplished—often judge their abilities not only more harshly but fundamentally *differently* than others do. On the flip side, gifted children grow up to be more vulnerable and less sure of themselves, even when they should be the most confident people in the room.

Understanding *why* this happens is the first step in realizing your potential and avoiding the pitfalls that have derailed you in the past. The second step is to learn how you can change your own mind-set—the one you didn't even realize you had—and learn to see your work and your world through a new, more inspiring, and more accurate lens.

YOUR OWN TOUGHEST CRITIC

When I was a graduate student at Columbia University, my mentor, Carol Dweck, and another student, Claudia Mueller, conducted a study looking at the effects of different kinds of praise on fifth graders.[4] They were interested in how praise can influence your beliefs about what you can and cannot do, and how you deal with the difficulties and setbacks that happen down the road. All the students in their study began by getting a relatively easy set of problems to solve and were then praised for their performance. Half of them were given praise that emphasized their natural ability ("You did really well. You must be really smart!"). The other half were praised instead for their strong effort ("You did really well. You must have worked really hard!").

Next, each student was given a very difficult set of problems—so difficult, in fact, that few students got even one answer correct. All were told that this time they had "done a lot worse." Finally, they were given a third set of easy problems—as easy as the first set had been—in order to see how experiencing failure would affect their performance.

Dweck and Mueller found that children who were praised for their "smartness" did roughly 25 percent worse on the final set of problems compared with how they did on the first set. They were more likely to blame their poor performance on a lack of ability; consequently, they enjoyed working on the problems less and gave up on them sooner.

Children who had been praised for their effort, on the other hand, performed roughly 25 percent better on the final set of problems compared with the first. They blamed their difficulty on *not having tried hard enough*; as a result, they persisted longer on the final set of problems and even enjoyed the experience.

It's important to remember that in Dweck and Mueller's study, there were no differences in ability on average between the kids in the "smart" praise and "effort" praise groups—everyone did well on the first set, and everyone had difficulty on the second set. The only difference was how the two groups were led to *interpret* the difficulty they experienced—what it meant to them when the problems were hard to solve. "Smart" praise kids were much quicker to doubt their ability, to lose confidence, and to perform less effectively as a result.

The kind of feedback we get from parents, teachers, and mentors when we are young has a major impact on the beliefs we develop about our abilities—including whether we see them as innate and unchangeable or as capable of developing through effort and practice. Telling a young artist that she is "so creative," "so talented," or "has such a gift" implies that creativity and talent are qualities you either have or you don't. The net result: when a project doesn't turn out so well, or the artist's work is rejected, she takes it as evidence that she isn't very "creative" or "talented" after all, rather than seeing the feedback as a sign that she needs to dig deeper, try harder, or find a new approach.

TWO MIND-SETS: BE GOOD VS. GET BETTER

We all approach the goals we pursue with one of two mind-sets: what

I call the Be Good mind-set, where the focus is on proving that you already have a lot of ability and that you know exactly what you're doing, and the Get Better mind-set, where the focus is on developing your ability and learning new skills. You can think of it as the difference between wanting to show that you *are* smart versus wanting to actually get smarter.

When we have a Be Good mind-set, we are constantly comparing our performance with that of other people's, to see how we size up and to receive validation for our talents. This is the mind-set we end up with when we are given too much "ability" praise and come to believe that our talents are innate and unchanging. It's also the mind-set we often (unconsciously) adopt when our environment is highly evaluative—when our work is constantly exposed to the judgment of others. For creative professionals, this is particularly the case—evaluation and criticism are an unavoidable part of any artist's life.

The problem with the Be Good mind-set is that it leaves us vulnerable when things get hard or when the people we compare ourselves with are excelling. We quickly start to doubt our ability ("Oh no, maybe I'm *not* good at this!"), and this creates a lot of anxiety. Ironically, worrying about your ability makes you much more likely to ultimately fail. Countless studies have shown that nothing interferes with your performance quite like anxiety does—it is *the* creativity killer.

A Get Better mind-set, on the other hand, leads instead to self-comparison and a concern with making progress: How well am I doing today, compared with how I did yesterday, last month, or last year? Are my talents and abilities developing over time? Am I moving closer to becoming the creative professional I want to be?

The great thing about the Get Better mind-set is that it is practically bulletproof. When we think about what we are doing in terms of learning and improving, accepting that we may make some mistakes along the way, we stay motivated and persist despite the setbacks that might occur. We also find the work we do more interesting and enjoyable, and experience less depression and anxiety. We procrastinate less and plan better. We feel more creative and innovative. And we remember why we wanted to do this for a living in the first place.

SHIFTING YOUR MIND-SET

How can you retrain your brain and adopt the Get Better mind-set at work and in life?

1. **Give yourself permission to screw up.** I can't emphasize enough how important this is. Start any new project or endeavor by saying to yourself, "I may not get the hang of this right away. I'm going to make mistakes, and that's okay."

People get very nervous when I tell them to embrace the mistake. But they shouldn't be, because as studies in my lab and others have shown, when people are allowed to make mistakes, they are significantly less likely to actually make them. Often, when we tackle a new project, we expect to be able to do the work flawlessly no matter how challenging it might be. The focus is all about Being Good, and the prospect becomes daunting. The irony is that all this pressure to Be Good results in many more mistakes, and far inferior performance, than would a focus on Getting Better.

2. Ask for help when you run into trouble. Needing help doesn't mean you aren't capable—in fact, the opposite is true. Only the very foolish believe they can do everything on their own. And studies show that asking for help when you need it actually makes people think you are more capable, not less.

3. Compare your performance today with your performance last week or last year, rather than comparing yourself with other people. I know that you can't really avoid comparing yourself with others entirely, but when you catch yourself doing it, remind yourself that this kind of thinking doesn't get you anywhere. What matters is that you are moving forward and improving over time.

4. Think in terms of progress, not perfection. It can be helpful to write down your goals in whatever way you usually think of them— odds are you think of them in a Be Good way—and then rewrite them using Get Better language: words like *improve, learn, progress, develop, grow,* and *become.* For example:

> *Your Be Good Goal: I want to be good at marketing my own work.*
>
> *The Get Better Version: I will develop my ability to market my own work and become a more effective marketer.*

5. Examine your beliefs and, when necessary, challenge them. No matter what kind of learning opportunities you are given, you probably aren't going to see lasting improvement if—deep down—you don't believe improvement is possible. Believing that your abilities are fixed is a self-fulfilling prophecy, and the self-doubt it creates will sabotage you in the end. Whether it's intelligence, creativity, self-control, charm, or athleticism—the science shows our abilities to be profoundly malleable. When it comes to mastering any skill, your experience, effort, and persistence matter a lot. Change really *is* always possible—there is no ability that can't be developed with effort. So the next time you find yourself thinking, "But I'm just not good at this," remember: you're just not good at it *yet*.

DR. HEIDI GRANT HALVORSON *is a researcher, author, speaker, and associate director of Columbia Business School's Motivation Science Center. She blogs for 99U,* Harvard Business Review, Fast Company, *the* Wall Street Journal, *and the* Huffington Post. *Her books include* Succeed, Nine Things Successful People Do Differently, *and* Focus.

→ www.heidigranthalvorson.com

"Work to become,

not to acquire."

DEVELOPING MASTERY THROUGH DELIBERATE PRACTICE

—

Tony Schwartz

It's a small study—just thirty subjects, probably not enough to be statistically significant—but it contains incredibly rich information about the pursuit of mastery and the ingredients of great performance.

K. Anders Ericsson, arguably the world's leading expert on performance, conducted the study with thirty young violinists attending the Music Academy of West Berlin, one of the most selective conservatories in the world. Ericsson's aim was to understand, at the most granular level, not just what these talented musicians had in common but what set them apart from their colleagues. In short, what practices led them to the highest level of excellence?

Ericsson's core finding is now the stuff of legend: namely that it takes ten thousand hours of what he calls "deliberate practice" to achieve true mastery in any skilled pursuit. Nothing less will do, but it's possible for nearly anyone to reach excellence in nearly anything, given sufficient persistence and expert feedback along the way. This finding is the core tenet of Malcolm Gladwell's bestselling *Outliers*, and it's been cited in dozens of other books and articles, but it's actually only a small part of what the study revealed.

Practice undeniably lies at the heart of mastery. In Ericsson's study, he divided the violinists into three groups based on their level of skill as measured by their teachers. The lowest level group practiced slightly less than ninety minutes a day. The top two groups both practiced an average of approximately four hours a day, in sessions no longer than ninety minutes, after which they took a break. The only notable difference in the training of the two groups was that the top ones had started playing violin at a younger age and therefore had accumulated more hours of practice than those in the second group.

But why, as more mature musicians, did they practice in almost exactly the same way? And why is that approach also characteristic of the highest achievers among athletes, chess players, writers, and scientists, among others?

The answer is rooted in our physiology. We human beings are designed to move between spending and renewing energy. We're at our best when we align with our internal rhythms. That means sleeping at night and being awake during the day. At night, we sleep in something called the Basic Rest Activity cycle—five stages, from light to deep sleep and back out again approximately every ninety minutes. This same cycle recapitulates itself during the day, except we move every ninety minutes from high physiological alertness progressively down into a state of fatigue.

The musicians in Ericsson's study were almost certainly unaware of these facts, but the best among them tuned into the signals from their own bodies. Nearly all those in the top two groups began practice first thing in the morning, when their energy was the highest and the number of distractions they faced the lowest. When they began to feel tired, as they approached ninety minutes, they rested and renewed. After three such sessions, they were spent for the day. Ericsson subsequently posited that four and a half hours is the natural human limit for the highest level of focus on a single task in any given day.

WHAT WE CAN LEARN FROM THE SCIENCE OF HIGH PERFORMANCE

Embedded in these findings are powerful and highly specific lessons for anyone seeking mastery. The first one has to do with the power of ritual. A ritual is a highly precise behavior you do at a specific time so that it becomes automatic over time and no longer requires much conscious intention or energy.

Will and discipline, it turns out, are highly overrated. We each have one reservoir we draw on, and it gets progressively depleted each time we use it to get something done. If we spend energy when we wake up deciding what to wear that day, or completing a difficult task in the morning, or resisting a chocolate chip cookie following lunch, we're left with less energy to complete any subsequent task. A ritualized approach to practice helps conserve our precious and finite reserves of energy.

The second mastery lesson from Ericsson's violinists is that the best way to practice is in time-limited sprints, rather than for an unbounded number of hours. It's far less burdensome to mobilize attention on a task if you've got clear starting and stopping points. The ability to focus single-mindedly lies at the heart of mastering any challenge. Time-limited sessions also make it easier to tolerate abstaining from distractions such as e-mail and social media.

The third key to mastery is perhaps the most counter-intuitive. It's the importance of restoration. Many of us fear that taking time for rest and renewal will brand us as slackers. More, bigger, faster, for longer, remains the prevailing ethic in most corporate cultures. In fact, rest is a critical component of achieving sustainable excellence over time.

This insight leads to one that's even more surprising. When Ericsson asked the subjects in his study to name the second most important factor in improving as violinists, the near-unanimous answer was sufficient sleep. Both the top two groups slept an average of 8.5 hours out of every 24—including a twenty- to thirty-minute nap in the midafternoon. The least skilled group still slept 7.8 hours a night. The average American, by contrast, sleeps an average of 6 to 6.5 hours a night. Sleep not only serves a restorative purpose but also allows the brain to more effectively consolidate and retain daytime learning. The top violinists recognized this intuitively, and slept accordingly.

CREATING A PERSONAL RITUAL FOR DELIBERATE PRACTICE

I know this approach works, not only because I've taught it to thousands of people over the past ten years and seen the results but also because it's the way I've learned to work far more effectively on my own projects.

For many years, I wrote books by sitting down at my desk in the morning and staying there all day long without specific breaks. I constantly fought distraction, couldn't focus very well, and frequently ended my days feeling physically and mentally exhausted and disappointed with my output.

It was only after I began studying the science of high performance that I started building a new sort of practice ritual. I still sit down at my desk first thing in the morning when I'm working on books, but now I write for exactly ninety minutes at a time—not eighty-five and not ninety-five. Then I take a break. I may get something to eat, close my eyes and spend ten minutes breathing deeply, or take a run, each activity in order to refuel and recover.

When I'm finished renewing, I come back and work the same way for another ninety minutes, before taking a second renewal break. After that, I return to my desk for one final ninety-minute session, and then I have lunch—another form of energy renewal. If it's been a particularly demanding day, I take a short nap. During the afternoon, I work on much less demanding tasks. The deliberate practice I've ritualized is intrinsically rewarding. I feel accomplished—and restored—even when the work doesn't translate immediately into external benefits. But it reliably produces benefits over the longer term.

During the years I sat at my desk struggling to focus all day long, each of my books took at least a year to write. Working less than half the number of hours each day, at a much higher level of focus, I've completed each of my last two books in less than six months. At least equally important, the quality of my thinking and writing—my sense of mastery—has dramatically increased.

It's unrealistic for most of us to set aside four and a half uninterrupted hours a day to do anything. Assuming that's so, consider starting with a smaller practice. What's the skill that you wish to develop the most? Keep in mind that you'll be immeasurably more motivated if it's something to which you're drawn deeply.

Next, set aside one uninterrupted period of, say, sixty minutes each working day to build the skill you've chosen, preferably first thing in the morning. As your capacity for focus grows stronger over time, add fifteen minutes, and then another fifteen minutes, until you reach ninety.

Consider building a similar practice, in reverse, around sleep. If you're currently getting fewer than seven hours—the minimum all but about 2.5 percent of us need to be fully rested—experiment by going to sleep a half hour earlier for the next week. Monitor how you feel as a result. If you're deriving daytime benefits, add fifteen minutes in the second week, and fifteen minutes more in the third.

The heart of achieving mastery, I've come to believe, is expanding the amplitude of the waves you make in your life. When you're working, give it everything you've got, for relatively short periods of time. When you're recovering, let go and truly refuel.

Average is a steady state, free of highs or lows. Unfortunately, average isn't very satisfying. Mastery is about regularly pushing yourself beyond your comfort zone, while also learning how to deeply restore and take care of yourself. Make rhythmic waves and you'll not only get better at what you practice, you'll also feel more in control of your life.

TONY SCHWARTZ *is the president and CEO of The Energy Project, a company that helps organizations fuel sustainable high performance by better meeting the needs of their employees. Tony's most recent books,* Be Excellent at Anything *and* The Power of Full Engagement *(coauthored with Jim Loehr), were both* New York Times *bestsellers.*

→ www.theenergyproject.com

"An ounce of practice is generally worth more than a ton of theory."

— E. F. SCHUMACHER

Q&A:

LEARNING TO LIVE OUTSIDE YOUR COMFORT ZONE

—

with Joshua Foer

Bestselling author Joshua Foer is not the type of writer to quietly observe from the sidelines. After covering the USA Memory Championship in 2005, Foer became fascinated with its strange world of memorization challenges (speed cards, facial recognition, poetry recitation) and decided to become an expert mnemonist himself. In 2006, he succeeded, winning the speed cards category handily by memorizing a deck of cards in one minute and forty seconds. During his training period, Foer studied with the British Grand Master of Memory, Ed Cooke, and researched how top performers—from memory champs to athletes to surgeons—acquire new skills. We chatted with Foer about why pushing through the "OK Plateau" is essential to building expertise over time.

What are the stages of skill acquisition?

In the 1960s, psychologists identified three stages that we pass through in the acquisition of new skills. We start in the "cognitive phase," during which we're intellectualizing the task, discovering new strategies to perform better, and making lots of mistakes. We're consciously focusing on what we're doing. Then we enter the "associative stage," when we're making fewer errors, and gradually getting better. Finally, we arrive at the "autonomous stage," when we turn on autopilot and move the skill to the back of our proverbial mental filing cabinet and stop paying it conscious attention.

Can you explain the concept of the OK Plateau?

The OK Plateau is that point when we reach the autonomous stage and consciously or unconsciously say to ourselves, "I am OK at how good I have gotten at this task," and stop paying conscious attention to our improvement. We all reach OK Plateaus in almost everything we do. We learn to drive when we're teenagers, and at first we improve rapidly, but eventually we are no longer a threat to old ladies crossing the street, and we stop getting appreciably better.

There are some generalizable principles that all experts use to push beyond the OK Plateau. Can you describe them?

Psychologists have studied experts in just about every possible field you can imagine, from athletics to the arts to business. They've found a surprisingly generalizable set of principles that tend to be used by experts in field after field. Those principles help explain why their practice results in their achieving the degree of expertise that others don't necessarily achieve. One of the essential things they have found is that, if you want to get better at something, you cannot do it in that autonomous stage. You can't get better on autopilot. One thing that experts in field after field tend to do is use strategies to keep themselves *out* of that autonomous stage and under their conscious direction. That's how you conquer those OK Plateaus.

So experts make sure they're staying in that early learning phase all the time?

Something experts in all fields tend to do when they're practicing is to operate outside of their comfort zone and study themselves failing. The best figure skaters in the world spend more of their practice time practicing jumps that they don't land than lesser figure skaters do. The same is true of musicians. When most musicians sit down to practice, they play the parts of pieces that they're good at. Of course they do: it's fun to succeed. But expert musicians tend to focus on the parts that are hard, the parts they haven't yet mastered. The way to get better at a skill is to force yourself to practice just beyond your limits.

How much time are these experts spending on practice? Is it about long hours? Or more about focusing on the right stuff?

There's no way to get good at anything without putting in the hours. But just as important as the quantity of time is the quality of time. If you're not being rigorous with your practice and focusing on the hard parts, you will improve very slowly.

How have you focused on the "hard stuff" as a writer over the course of your career?

I try to take on stories that really force me to push myself. For example, my current book project has required me to spend large amounts of time living in the Congolese rain forest with Babenjele pygmies. Every day out there is a challenge. But if you're not pushing yourself, how do you expect to grow?

What role does gathering feedback play?

Experts crave and thrive on immediate and constant feedback. One illustration of this can be found in the field of medicine. You might think that the longer a doctor has been practicing, the better she'll be. But there's one field of medicine where that seems not to be the case: mammography. Doctors who conduct mammographic screenings for cancer don't tend to make better predictions the longer they've been practicing. Surgeons, on the other hand, tend to get better with time. The difference lies in the feedback. With mammographic screenings, it might be weeks, months, or years before a doctor finds out whether her diagnosis was accurate or she missed a tumor. A surgeon, on the other hand, gets immediate and precise feedback: the patient either gets better or doesn't. There's a practical suggestion here: doctors who do mammographic screenings should be regularly tested with old screenings so that they can get that immediate feedback and learn from it.

What did you learn from your memory coach?

Ed Cooke has one of the best-trained memories in Europe. I couldn't have become the United States Memory Champion without him. He forced me to practice, and he gave me constant feedback about how I could improve my performance.

Do you think that you can coach yourself equally well?

It's hard to be your own coach, but not impossible. The key thing is to set up structures that provide you with objective feedback—and to not be so blind that you can't take that feedback and use it.

Sometimes a mentor or coach isn't available. How do you set up feedback systems in that situation?

When I was training my memory, I kept meticulous spreadsheets to track my performance. They allowed me to see what was working and what wasn't. Numbers don't lie.

Continuously operating outside your comfort zone is a tall order. Any advice on how to stay motivated to push yourself?

It helps to have a strong, clear vision of where you're going. When things get hard, you need to be able to see the reward that awaits at the end of all the struggle.

JOSHUA FOER is the author of the international bestseller Moonwalking with Einstein: The Art and Science of Remembering Everything. *His writing has appeared in the* New Yorker, National Geographic, Esquire, *the* New York Times, *and other publications. He is the co-founder of* Atlas Obscura *and* Sukkah City.

→ www.joshuafoer.com

"In a time of
drastic change,
it is the learners
who inherit the
future."

— ERIC HOFFER

REPROGRAMMING YOUR DAILY HABITS

–

Scott H. Young

What did you do yesterday? If you're like most people, you'll probably try to answer that by focusing on the decisions you made. Maybe you decided to stay a bit longer at work, or to knock off early. Maybe you decided to tackle a tricky problem or confront your boss about a nagging issue. Conscious decisions like these stick out in our minds because we put effort into making them.

But how did you decide what to eat for breakfast yesterday? Or which route to take to work? Chances are, there wasn't much of a decision at all. You ate the breakfast you normally eat. You commuted to work the way you always do.

If you think hard about it, you'll notice just how many "automatic" decisions you make each day. But these habits aren't always as trivial as what you eat for breakfast. Your health, your productivity, and the growth of your career are all shaped by the things you do each day—most by habit, not by choice.

Even the choices you do make consciously are heavily influenced by automatic patterns. Researchers have found that our conscious mind is better understood as an explainer of our actions, not the cause of them. Instead of triggering the action itself, our consciousness tries to explain why we took the action after the fact, with varying degrees of success. This means that even the choices we do appear to make intentionally are at least somewhat influenced by unconscious patterns.

Given this, what you do every day is best seen as an iceberg, with a small fraction of conscious decision sitting atop a much larger foundation of habits and behaviors. But this view doesn't need to be pessimistic. Recognizing that most of our actions are controlled by habits can be powerful. Once you know that patterns run much of your life, you can start figuring out how to change them.

PROGRAMMING EFFECTIVENESS

About ten years ago, I noticed a problem in my life. I kept failing to keep the goals that I had set for myself. I would want to work hard on a project that was necessary for my business, but I'd fail to execute. Like most people, I blamed laziness or a lack of motivation for these failings.

But then I learned about habits. It turns out willpower is a finite resource—something that gets depleted with use. Roy Baumeister did the first experiments on this phenomenon, known as "ego deple-tion," showing that the exertion of willpower in one area makes it harder to exert it on another task later.[5]

This corresponded with what I had observed in myself. Each time I would put more effort into doing better at one task, I would fail with another. I felt like I was juggling all my activities and con-stantly dropping the balls.

Creating habits held a powerful allure. If I could take the will-power-draining activities I was failing to execute and gradually turn them into unconscious habits, I could then use the "tugboat" of my conscious willpower to work on something else.

HOW TO CHANGE A HABIT

The key to changing a habit is to realize the ineffectiveness of will-power. It's not that willpower is unnecessary, but more that it's a much less powerful tool than most of us assume. Because our will-power is limited, it helps to be clever in how we establish new habits.

Given this, I've found that it makes the most sense to invest heav-ily in the early phase of building a new habit so that, later, it will run automatically without calling on your resources of self-discipline. I call this the principle of focus, and it goes against the normal method people use when they want to change their behavior.

THE PRINCIPLE OF FOCUS

Focus means changing only one habit at a time. I've found it best to spend at least one month exclusively on one habit before moving to the next. For example, let's say you want to wake up earlier, exercise more often, and introduce a new organizational system at work. You recognize that your current habits for sleep, health, and work are slowing you down, and you want to make some positive changes.

If you're like most people, you'll start by tackling all three at once. This might even work, for a short time. But after a week or two, something will cause you to slip with one of these new activities. In the beginning you're relying entirely on willpower, so when a behavior slips, it goes back to the default behavior you had been using before.

A smarter strategy is to implement each new habit successively, focusing on just one new habit a month. The first month you focus on waking up earlier. The second month on regular exercise. The third month on a new system for your work. Although thirty days may not be enough time to form a new default habit (one study suggests sixty-six days as a median time for habituation[6]), it will at least mean the habit requires less effort to pick back up in case of a setback.

Some people might see this approach as being prohibitively slow, but in practice, doing habits one month at a time is fast. In one year you could:

- Wake up earlier

- Exercise regularly

- Eat properly

- Set up a productivity system

- Establish deliberate practice time for your craft

- Become more organized

- Read a book per month

- Cut out wasteful Internet surfing

- Keep your e-mail inbox empty

- Cut down on television

- Learn a new skill

- Maintain a journal or diary

Even if you only accomplished a quarter of this list, my guess is you could make significant gains in your life. The focus principle for habit change isn't actually slow. In fact, it's much faster than the alternative.

THE PRINCIPLE OF CONSISTENCY

The next insight for changing habits is called classical conditioning. This is a basic psychological principle first discovered by Ivan Pavlov through his famous experiment with dogs. Pavlov would ring a bell and then bring his dogs food. Soon enough, the dogs would salivate after hearing the bell, anticipating food. This salivation would continue even if the food never arrived, showing that the dogs automatically associated the sound of the bell with a meal. [7]

You can also use classical conditioning to speed up the process of habit change. By making the habit you're working on extremely consistent, you speed up the time it takes to make the behavior automatic.

This is the reason the dogs started to salivate when the bell was rung. Had Dr. Pavlov rang the bell only some of the time, or brought food based on different triggers, the dogs may not have made the association automatically.

Consistency means that you try to do a habit the same way each time. Imagine you wanted to set up a deliberate practice routine, where you work on a tough skill you're trying to master for your career. Let's say you want to commit to working on it for around three hours per week.

One way you could do this is to do one hour, three days per week, when you have time. Some days you might do it before work, other days after; sometimes on weekdays and sometimes on weekends. This may work, but it's hardly consistent. As a result, the habit will take a lot longer to become automatic.

Instead, imagine that you spent thirty-five minutes each day immediately after work on that skill. Now the behavior is very consistent. It takes place on the same days, in the same conditions, in exactly the same fashion. It won't be long before doing your practice routine after work becomes an automatic part of your day.

With focus and consistency you can change your habits. By changing your habits, you reprogram the behaviors that control most of your life and ultimately determine your success.

SCOTT H. YOUNG has been studying the science of learning, habit change, and meaningful productivity since he was seventeen. He has written numerous e-books, including Holistic Learning, which is available on his website.

→ www.scotthyoung.com/blog

"Change will lead to insight far more often than insight will lead to change."

— MILTON ERICKSON

KEEPING A DIARY TO CATALYZE CREATIVITY

—

Teresa Amabile, Steven Kramer
& Ela Ben-Ur

What does Andy Warhol have in common with World War II general George Patton? And what do they both have in common with revolutionary Che Guevara, design visionary Buckminster Fuller, and writer Virginia Woolf? All kept a diary or personal journal.

Interestingly, although diaries have been written by people in a staggering array of occupations, a disproportionate number of diarists were engaged in creative pursuits. *Wikipedia* lists 223 notable diarists; the primary occupation of fully half is a creative one. These include not only writers, for whom keeping a diary might seem a natural thing to do, but also painters, sculptors, scientists, architects, designers, musicians, and more. The great American photographer Edward Weston made regular entries in his *Daybooks* for nearly thirty years.

That's no coincidence. A diary can serve as a source of solace and inspiration, insight into emerging patterns, and motivation to reach new creative heights—if you know how to use it.

WHY KEEP A DIARY?

Creative people frequently work solo, without the benefit of colleagues who could help capture or develop their ideas. But even teams and organizations rarely offer creatives the necessary time, understanding, and patience to nurture their creative seedlings.

A diary can help fill the void. It can serve as a sounding board and an alter-ego companion—one who will never forget what you say. What might otherwise have been isolated or passing thoughts become permanent and potentially powerful ideas.

This sounding board can serve a number of functions, the simplest of which is planning. Many entries in *The Daybooks of Edward Weston* reveal him focusing on future actions to capitalize on emerging opportunities:

> *The excerpts from my daybook and photographs will be published in the August issue of* Creative Art. . . . *It seems my fortunes are to change for something better. Now I must spend all my spare time in cutting and correcting my manuscript.*
> *—Edward Weston, May 23, 1928*

Of course, Weston could have used a simple calendar or to-do list to plan next steps. But notice his remark that his luck seems to be changing. What a calendar cannot do, and a journal can, is help you reflect on the big picture of your life and your creative work—where it is, what it means, and what direction you want it to take.

Diaries can be particularly helpful tools for accurately capturing positive events. In his book, *Thinking, Fast and Slow*, the psychologist Daniel Kahneman distinguishes between experience and memory, noting that human memory of an experience can easily be altered. Kahneman describes a man who was enjoying a concert immensely until the very end, when there was an obnoxious sound in the concert hall. The man said that the noise ruined the entire concert for him. But it didn't really, of course; he had enjoyed the concert up until that moment. What it did ruin was his memory of the concert.

By keeping a daily diary, you will reduce the chance that some later event will transform your memory of the day's experiences. So when you feel you have accomplished something, write it down soon, before a client or critic has the opportunity to say something that diminishes that sense of progress.

This is one of the most important reasons to keep a diary: it can make you more aware of your own progress, thus becoming a wellspring of joy in your workday. In the following entry, Weston remarks on how his photographic technique is improving, allowing him to create his art more effectively and satisfyingly.

> *I believe I am not merely enthused in writing that*
> *these negatives are the most important I have ever*
> *done. . . . My technique matched my vision—two*
> *or three slightly overtimed, but printable without*
> *alteration. . . .*
> —Edward Weston, May 23, 1928

In our research into the diaries of more than two hundred professionals working on creative projects inside organizations, we found that the single most important motivator is making progress in meaningful work. On the days when these professionals saw themselves moving forward on something they cared about—even if the progress was a seemingly incremental "small win"—they were more likely to be happy and deeply engaged in their work. And, being happier and more deeply engaged, they were more likely to come up with new ideas and solve problems creatively. That's why Weston was so elated to note that "my technique matched my vision."

To hatch ideas big and small, and to make them happen, you need a mind clear of worry over "small stuff," a sense of progress and direction, and a broad perspective on your life as it unfolds. In the Journaling Cycle figure on the next page, we have summarized these functions (and others) that a diary can serve—if you really engage with it.

THE JOURNALING CYCLE

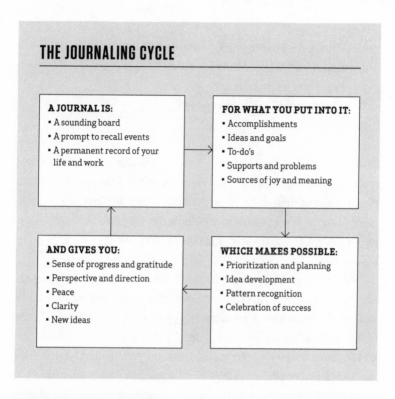

A JOURNAL IS:
- A sounding board
- A prompt to recall events
- A permanent record of your life and work

FOR WHAT YOU PUT INTO IT:
- Accomplishments
- Ideas and goals
- To-do's
- Supports and problems
- Sources of joy and meaning

AND GIVES YOU:
- Sense of progress and gratitude
- Perspective and direction
- Peace
- Clarity
- New ideas

WHICH MAKES POSSIBLE:
- Prioritization and planning
- Idea development
- Pattern recognition
- Celebration of success

HOW TO USE YOUR DIARY

Your diary can only function as a sounding board if you speak to it regularly—and then listen to it. For most of us, keeping a diary can be difficult, particularly at the start. Even some dedicated diarists, like nineteenth-century Scottish writer Sir Walter Scott, struggle to keep up with their entries:

> *Having omitted to carry on my diary for two or three days, I lost heart to make it up, and left it unfilled for many a month and day. . . .*
> —Sir Walter Scott, January 1, 1829

Establishing a simple journaling habit is the key; it gets easier and more self-motivating as you go. We recommend that you start small. Rather than vowing to do it for the rest of your life, make a commitment to write in your diary every single day for just one month. Skipping a day will make it easier to skip the next day, as Scott learned to his dismay.

Pick a time when you are likely to have ten minutes to yourself. Ideally, this will be the same time and place each day, to help build the habit. And create a memory trigger, so you won't forget. Some online journaling programs will send you a daily reminder. Or you might leave a diary notebook and pen on your bedside table. The medium is unimportant, as long as it's something you'll enjoy using.

Another obstacle is thinking of something to say. Sir Walter Scott continued the above diary entry:

> *During this period nothing has happened worth particular notice. The same occupations, the same amusements . . . I half grieve to take up my pen, and doubt if it is worth while to record such an infinite*

> *quantity of nothing. But hang it! I hate to be beat so*
> *here goes for better behavior!*
> —*Sir Walter Scott, January 1, 1829*

What should you write about, especially on those days that feel like "an infinite quantity of nothing" has happened? Write about anything that stands out as you reflect back on the day; unless you were unconscious the entire day, *something* happened.

There's no magic formula, as evidenced by the staggering variety of what renowned diarists focused on. But our research suggests that it can be particularly useful to reflect and write on any of the following:

- Progress, even a small step forward, in work you care about

- Anyone or anything that helped or hindered your progress

- Goals and plans, especially a plan for making progress tomorrow

- Issues or "to-dos" that may be causing you stress as they swirl through your mind

- Anything that brought you joy or pleasure, even if it lasted only a moment

Although the act of reflecting and writing, in itself, can be beneficial, you'll multiply the power of your diary if you review it regularly—if you listen to what your life has been telling you. Periodically, maybe once a month, set aside time to get comfortable and read back through your entries. And, on New Year's Day, make an annual ritual of reading through the previous year. We think you'll be impressed by the insights you'll get, particularly if you look for certain clues.

Be alert to emerging patterns, and jot them down as you see them. Was there a type of project on which you seemed to make particularly steady progress or feel particularly engaged? Specifically, try to identify the greatest sources of meaning in your work—the types of projects in which you felt you were really making a difference. Those are clues about what motivates you most strongly and where you should concentrate your energies going forward.

Was there an idea that looks promising—perhaps an idea that you had completely forgotten? This could signal that what you've learned since having that idea, or what's changed in the world around you, now makes it more viable and valuable.

Track improvements in your personal or professional self, improvements that may have been impossible to see from day to day. Seeing that progress can be powerfully motivating.

Look for recurring problems and hindrances, and plan to attack them. Focus on one short-term action—something you can do the next day—and one longer-term action—something you can do in the next month.

Finally, allow yourself a few moments to feel grateful for the skills you've developed and the people who have helped you. Bask in the glow of your accomplishments. This is your life; savor it. Hold on to the threads across days that, when woven together, reveal the rich tapestry of what you are achieving and who you are becoming. The best part is that, seeing the story line appearing, you can actively create what it—and you—will become.

TERESA AMABILE is a professor and director of research at Harvard Business School and coauthor, with STEVEN KRAMER, of The Progress Principle. *They are psychologists who research what makes people happy, motivated, productive, and creative at work.*

→ www.progressprinciple.com

—

ELA BEN-UR is a thirteen-year IDEO veteran and a professor at Olin College. Through her firm, i2i Experience, she works as a human-centered design innovation coach and consultant.

→ www.i2iexperience.com

KEY
TAKEAWAYS
—

Building Expertise

Get more insights and the desktop wallpaper at:

→ www.99u.com/expertise

STOP TRYING TO "BE GOOD"

Give yourself permission to screw up. Once you stop trying to be good (and look smart), you can focus on tackling the exciting challenges that will help you get better.

SPRINT TO SPEED UP MASTERY

Set aside time for regular "sprints" where you work intensively on a key project or skill without distraction. Then reward yourself with a break.

AVOID THE "OK PLATEAU"

Focus on practicing the hard stuff when you're developing new skills. As with weight lifting, you know you're making headway when you feel the burn.

HUNGER FOR FEEDBACK

Develop a method for gathering feedback—whether it's tracking the numbers yourself or hiring a coach. No factor is more essential to growth and learning.

MAKE BUILDING HABITS A HABIT

Try to change one key habit a month. If you can make the behaviors that help you excel automatic, executing at the top of your game becomes significantly easier.

DAILY OBSERVATION DRIVES PROGRESS

Track your progress by journaling for a few minutes every day. The practice will help you identify stumbling blocks, observe patterns, and document successes.

CHAPTER THREE

CULTIVATING

RELATIONSHIPS

–

*How to build collaborative
alliances and networks that
will enrich your work*

As the poet John Donne wrote, "No man is an island." While we may cherish the myth of the lonely creative genius, it is just that— a myth. In truth, no individual (or idea) can flourish in a vacuum. Relationships, camaraderie, and collaboration are the lifeblood of our personal well-being and our professional success.

Put simply, opportunities flow through people. If you want a job, what you need is someone to hire you. If you want capital to start a business, what you need is an investor. If you want to sell a product, what you need is a customer. At every stage in our careers, whatever level of opportunity or growth we seek, we depend on relationships to drive us forward.

To achieve all that we're capable of, we must enlist a group of allies to accompany us on our journey, empower our coworkers and clients to give us honest feedback, build collaborative teams with an eye toward fresh perspectives, and tend to our network of acquaintances with generosity and authenticity.

In a world of collaborative creation, whom we surround ourselves with dictates how much we can achieve.

ASKING FOR HELP ON YOUR JOURNEY

—

Steffen Landauer

Many creative people see their work as primarily an individual endeavor. They consider the most valuable thing that others can do for them is to leave them alone. At times, of course, most of us do feel that way. After all, only one person can hold the pen or sit at the keyboard, and in the creative realm the best work often reflects a strong individual vision rather than a collective one.

As Albert Einstein wrote, "Everything that is really great and inspiring is created by the individual who can labor in freedom." Many creatives follow this edict in pursuing their own projects. But if this approach is followed too closely, we can miss out on valuable help that can advance our work.

Some years ago I signed up for a storytelling workshop led by Jay O'Callahan, a well-known storyteller. I had recently completed several extended trips through Africa, Asia, and Patagonia and was looking for help in how to shape these experiences into stories. A dozen people who didn't know one another showed up and spent a weekend working together on various small exercises or "sparks"—two minutes spent describing a certain type of experience you've had—and also telling stories we had prepared for the workshop. These stories ranged from personal narratives, such as my travel experiences, to traditional stories from all over the world. There was a great chemistry in the workshop and we decided to plan a reunion six months later. Another reunion followed and then another, and to the amazement of everyone in this chance group, we have just marked our twentieth anniversary with our fortieth meeting.

I am a rather unlikely member, as I have always felt leery of organized groups; I prefer interacting with individuals, and I enjoy spending time on my own. In fact, the stories I was trying to shape were based on three years of solo travel around the world. Reflecting on these twenty years of the storytelling group, however, I am struck by how helpful the group has been to me and to the other members.

This help has taken several different forms. On individual projects, usually stories, we have gotten invaluable guidance—help in an area where we have been blocked, or simply encouragement to continue where we have been struggling with something. Sometimes, however, the guidance is more direct and specific. I still remember how I was struggling to shape a story about my travels in Patagonia, and someone suggested that I was avoiding the most interesting aspect of my story, my own sense of fear and insignificance amid the vast and barren landscape.

I left our most recent gathering, as I leave most of our meetings, energized by the workshop and surprised by how much we are able to do for one another. Then I started wondering why more of this does not happen through the normal course of life, particularly among people who have projects they are passionate to pursue. Is it that we are simply not that interested in helping others in their work? That we are not capable of help? Or that we are simply afraid to ask?

My own day-to-day work is in the corporate world, with responsibility for maximizing learning for a large global company. In most ways the work is quite different from a storytelling workshop, yet I have found a surprising number of parallels. In particular, there is one common question of central importance: How can we best realize the value that others can add to the development of our projects and ourselves?

In the corporate sphere, there is increasing appreciation for the role that others can play. One sign of this is the proliferation of executive coaching, the basic premise of which is that others have a critical role to play in helping us reach our potential. These others can either be professional coaches, peer coaches, or simply anybody who can offer you useful feedback. The prevalence of 360-degree feedback is one example, in which the company solicits those who work most closely with you to offer advice in how you can reach your potential.

Many of those in the creative world, however, spend much of their time working on their own and will never be assigned a coach or given regular feedback. For these individuals, here are a few actions worth considering in order to enlist the help of others:

1. Seek fellow travelers. There was a strong hand of serendipity in how our storytelling group came together, but there is no need to rely on chance in finding those who can help you. It may be that you need to get over an obstacle on a particular project, in which case you will need to get as specific as you can about the help you are looking for and who would be best positioned to offer it. It may also be that you are looking for broader advice about exploring a new creative direction. Regardless of your needs, there is one quality that is especially important in choosing fellow travelers: Will they tell you the truth? There are many reasons why people may fail this test—the quality of your relationship, their position in the organization, their personality traits—but many perfectly nice individuals, with whom you could enjoy a drink or a dinner, may not be ideal helpers. Get very concrete about the help you are seeking and learn to "audition" people until you find what you need.

2. Ask for help. This can be very difficult for people who see creative work as a solitary pursuit and any request for assistance as some combination of laziness or cowardice. If you think along these lines, and are able to overcome it, you are likely to encounter two surprises: first, people in general will be willing to help and, second, that help will be far more useful than you might have imagined. In any case, the first step is to ask. The worst that can happen is that someone will say no or will offer suggestions that are not especially helpful and can be ignored.

3. Build a structure for collaboration. This can take care of itself if a single meeting serves your needs. However, a broader engagement is often helpful. Our storytelling group developed a regular twice-a-year meeting structure, which has worked well for us. Beyond that, several substructures were also developed within the group. Two group members meet on a biweekly basis for ninety-minute coaching sessions, split evenly so each individual can be coached by the other. This format has survived for many years because each found it so helpful. For professional executive coaches, the structure is often a regular monthly schedule of meetings. The point is that some regular structure for the collaboration is often helpful, unless of course you are the type who simply cannot bear structure, in which case a basic arrangement to "call when one of us could use a view or an ear" can also work well.

4. Consider yourselves "accountability partners." There are several important points here. First, it requires a fellow traveler who is willing to hold you accountable, which means to help you establish milestones in a project and remind you of them or help you reach them as needed. Second, it implies a partnership, as the most enduring of these arrangements involve some reciprocity, though not necessarily within a given meeting or even a given month. Finally, note that strong partnerships are often based on contrasting rather than coinciding strengths, so you'll want to avoid the comfortable trap of seeking someone too similar to yourself. In Plato's *Republic*, guards were taught by poets. Views contrary to your own are always helpful, as sometimes you will see truth in them and effect change, and, if not, you will be stress-testing and ultimately strengthening your own convictions.

5. Highlight and discuss strengths. Often the most helpful thing that can be expressed, as specifically as possible, is what is strong and working well within a project. In our storytelling group, the first feedback round is always framed as an "appreciation" and targeted only at what listeners liked best about the piece. This format is designed to counter our tendency to focus initially on what needs to be fixed or what could be better. Often the path toward optimization for a story, or a project, or—notably—an individual is toward greater awareness and expansion of strengths.

One of the most powerful learnings I've had from twenty years of storytelling meetings spent shaping and helping others shape their stories is the realization of one's own power as a creator—not of a story, or of any project, but of the narrative of one's own creative life. The narratives of many creative people position their work as exclusively an individual pursuit. To ensure that you are optimizing your potential, consider recasting this narrative: Are you taking best advantage of the help that others can offer, and, more important, are you offering to others all the help you are capable of providing?

STEFFEN LANDAUER, when he is not telling stories,
and sometimes when he is, serves as Chief Learning
Officer for Citigroup, based in New York. He has held
similar roles focused on leadership development for
Hewlett-Packard and Goldman Sachs. His mission is to
enable learning.

→ www.linkedin.com/in/steffenlandauer

"If you want to go fast, go alone.

If you want to go far, go with others."

BUILDING RESILIENT RELATIONSHIPS

—

Michael Bungay Stanier

It always starts out so well. You've hired a new member of the team, you've joined a new project group, you've started working with a supplier. New people, new beginnings. And you're both up for it. "This," everyone's sure, "is the start of something cool/big/fun/productive . . . and above all, successful."

But inevitably, things shift. The person you've hired isn't as fast/ smart/experienced as you'd imagined. Your new boss reveals his or her obsessive/quirky/flawed character. The supplier starts breaking the promises you're sure they made. Whatever the situation, there are universal stumbling blocks:

- They misunderstand, you misunderstand

- They do too much or too little, you do too much or too little

- They overstep the boundaries, you overstep the boundaries

- They fall into unproductive patterns, you fall into unproductive patterns

- They go crazy, you go crazy

It's not "if." It's only ever "when." There's never been a relationship that didn't start off strongly and that didn't then run off the rails at some stage.

This is actually not the problem. This is just life. Success for you lies in managing these dips when they occur. It's not about having perfect relationships. That's a fantasy. It's about laying foundations for resilient relationships from the very start.

THE HOW VS. THE WHAT

Your best chance of bouncing back, sorting it out, and getting things rocking again lies in the practice of social contracting, a discipline that management thinker Peter Block introduced in his terrific book *Flawless Consulting*.

At the heart of social contracting is spending time up front talking about the How—the relationship and *how* we'll work together—rather than being seduced by the What, the excitement and urgency of the content, *what* needs to be sorted out and solved.

Just understanding that you should talk about the How will immediately make a difference in your working relationships. But to make it easier, here are five fundamental questions to ask and answer. You don't need to ask them all. I'm sure you'll find your own best combination for the person and the situation. Just make sure you ask some of them before things get rolling.

You'll want to remember that any good contract is a mutual exchange. So don't be fooled into thinking that your job is just to ask the questions. You need to be willing to answer them as well, so you and your collaborator both know where you each might stumble.

What do you want? (Here's what I want.) This is a question that almost always stops people in their tracks. It's deceptively difficult to answer and incredibly powerful when you can define clearly what exactly it is you want from this relationship.

Of course you'll want to articulate the transactional nature of things: I want you to get this done and get that completed. But see if you can go beyond that. What else do you want? ("I want this to position me for my next promotion.") What else would make this relationship one to truly value? ("I want this to lay the foundations of future work together.")

Where might you need help? (Here's where I'll need help.) This turns the "What do you want?" question over and comes at it from a different angle. You might want to specify where you'll trip yourself up (bold), how you might fall short in the relationship (bolder), or even how you might get in the way of success (boldest).

I'm forever telling people I'm going to need their help defining a better brief, not being a bottleneck on decisions, and staying interested in the minutiae of a project.

When you had a really good working relationship in the past, what happened? (Here's what happened for me.) Tell a story of a time when you were in a working relationship similar to this one, and it was good, really good. What did they do? What did you do? What else happened? What were the key moments when the path divided and you took one road and not the other? What else contributed to its success?

To take this to an even more courageous place, you can ask, "How do you feel about the amount of control you have over what we're trying to do here?" It's a question that shines a light into what is often a very dark corner: how control and power is working in the relationship.

When things go wrong, what does that look like on your end? How do you behave? (Here's how I behave.) Tell another story, this time of when a working relationship like this one failed to soar. It might be when it all went hellishly wrong or it might be when it disintegrated into mediocrity. What did you do and what did they do? Where were the missed opportunities? Where were the moments when things got broken?

Articulate, if you can, the unilateral actions you take when things start going wrong. Do you retreat into silence? Rage on? Try to take control and start to micromanage? Dump and run?

See also if you can summarize your own "hot buttons." What are the little things that can wind you up? Is it not getting replies to your e-mails? When others are late to meetings? Not having a regular check-in? Being given advice before you've got to the heart of the question? Spelling mistakes and random apostrophes? We've all got our pet peeves. If they know yours and you know theirs, things might be a little less frustrating.

When things go wrong—as they inevitably will—how shall we manage that? The power in this is twofold. First, you're acknowledging reality: Things will go wrong. Honeymoons end. Promises get broken. Expectations don't get met. By putting that on the table, you're able now to discuss what the plan will be when it does go wrong.

I've done everything from creating a code phrase ("I need to have an 'off my chest' conversation with you . . . ") to inventing a process ("I'm hitting the Mission Pause button"), to simply agreeing that we have permission to talk about things when we feel we must.

QUESTIONS ARE MORE POWERFUL THAN ANSWERS

What you hear and what you'll share will be interesting, insightful, and useful. But the irony is, the actual answers aren't the most important thing in this conversation. More powerful is the fact that by asking these questions you now have permission to acknowledge the situation between you both when things get off track (as they inevitably will). Talking about the How now allows you to talk about the How later, when the What is starting to go wrong.

That said, this is not a conversation most people have. Because it's not a conversation that just naturally happens. Someone—that would be you—has to have the courage to stop the usual flow, step aside for a moment, and begin this conversation. You may well pay the price of a slightly awkward conversation, possibly a couple of awkward conversations.

If you're just beginning a new working relationship, then you're in the perfect place to build in resilience through social contracting right now. And if, as is more likely, you've already got a number of working relationships—with your boss, with your team, with your customer, with your suppliers—you're also in the perfect place to build in resilience. Step back for a moment from the What you're all absorbed with, and invite them to have a conversation with you about the How.

MICHAEL BUNGAY STANIER is the senior partner and founder of Box of Crayons, a company that helps organizations do less Good Work and more Great Work. His books include Do More Great Work and the philanthropic project, End Malaria.

→ www.boxofcrayons.biz

"Everything that irritates us about others can lead us to an understanding of ourselves."

— CARL JUNG

Q&A:

NETWORKING IN A CONNECTION ECONOMY

—

with Sunny Bates

Sunny Bates is the ultimate super-connector. For more than twenty-five years, she has been a strategic adviser, curator, and connector for companies ranging from Kickstarter and TechStars to GE and TED. If "the medium is the message," her medium is people. She believes that whom you surround yourself with—and how you connect with them—is the single most important factor in unlocking your growth potential. We spoke with Sunny about the key stumbling blocks that keep people from making the right connections and how to approach the delicate art of network cultivation with a mind-set of generosity rather than obligation.

What do people struggle with the most when it comes to connecting with others and building a network?

Asking. Nobody ever wants to ask—at every level, with every kind of person, from the CEO all the way down. I think people get very narrow-minded, thinking that they can only reach out to people who are already doing a similar type of job. But the underlying network science says that it's all about weak links. Those people who are the friend of a friend of a friend. That's a much more likely place for something important to happen to you than your inner circle of close friends and colleagues.

What do you tell people who are afraid to ask?

If you don't ask, you'll never get. Sure, you may only get a little bit at a time. But if you don't ask, 100 percent of the time you won't get. You've just got to get over yourself. We live in a connection economy. If you can't connect with people for them to understand what you have to offer, you're working in a vacuum and you're going to lose out. You end up getting bitter in that situation, because you see your peers are moving up and doing things, and you say, "I could be doing those things. Why not me?"

It's very easy to think that somebody knows you. And that if they know you, they will think about calling you, or asking you, or wanting you for something. But people forget. I was a headhunter for many years, and I was always amazed because easily 20 percent of the time, the final person who was hired was well-known to the client. (They just hadn't thought about them.) That means that, for every five people you know, one is likely to have an impact on you or hire you—that should make you want to expand your circle.

What would you say to people who think that networking is somehow disingenuous or too transactional?

The underlying spirit of networking is generosity. If you engage with people in the spirit of generosity, as opposed to tit for tat—"I gave you three things, now you give me three things"—you'll go so much farther. What's more, the process can become joyful rather than an onerous task. Building a network is like cultivating a botanical garden: You don't want everyone in your network to be one color or one species. You want a variety of ages and stages and professions and passions, and to tend them carefully.

Do you have any particular strategies for reaching out to people?

Look at the people whom you admire most in your field. And literally map it out. Here are the four people that are doing great work at the organizations I respect. And just reach out. If you decided to contact one person a week, that would be fifty-two new people in a year. And it starts with that, just reaching out to someone because you admire their work, or are inspired by it. I've never met a person, no matter how well-known, who hasn't been flattered by an authentic compliment. Professional love letters work.

How do you maintain the relationship from there?

You always want to be specific about what you're asking for. Are you asking for a relationship? Are you asking for advice? Are you asking to follow up with them along the way, and occasionally reach out with a question? I think the best gauge for what's fair to ask is flipping the tables: How would you feel if somebody approached you and asked this exact same thing? If you feel okay with it, then go ahead and do it. If you feel a little uncomfortable, then try to tweak it in a way that makes you feel okay about it.

What if I really want to get to know them, beyond just a cup of coffee?

Particularly when you're thinking about creatives, there are a lot of people who have a day job at, say, an advertising agency, but their side projects are really what they care about most. If you can identify what that thing is, you have a chance to connect at the heart of what they care about.

Often, people try to connect in a more LinkedIn-type of scenario: "Oh, we have the same job" or "We do the same thing, so we should know each other." And the response that comes back is

often: "No, actually we don't do the same thing and I hate my job."
[Laughs.]

What about giving back to the people who have helped you?

People have this notion that they should always ask, "Is there anything I can do to help you?" to demonstrate a sort of reciprocity when they're asking for a favor or a connection. And it's very nice for someone to ask that—it's important—but you want to do it in an authentic way. I always appreciate when people ask in a way that's somehow embedded in the conversation rather than as an add-on at the very end. Like, "Oh, you gave me this, and so I have to ask you." It's always good to try to steer the exchange away from debt and obligation and more into the spirit of generosity.

Is there anything else to be aware of when you're thinking about networking in the creative world in particular?

In the creative world, there is a lot of love for the shiny penny. People are attracted to what's new and are quick to leave behind what's tried-and-true in favor of what's getting attention. I think that's interesting fodder for how you think about intentionally building your network for the long term. You want to focus on pulling in people whom you respect, people who you believe will have your interests in mind for the long haul, and also people across a wide enough range—so that you won't have to go back to the well over and over again with just a few people. If you build your network in a smart way, you can build your entire career on the back of it.

SUNNY BATES operates wherever executives, thinkers, artists, creators, innovators, entrepreneurs, educators, and philanthropists connect and collide around the globe. An expert in human network development, she has a client roster that includes some of the world's most prominent organizations, from Kickstarter and TED to GE and Credit Suisse to MTV, the National Academy of Sciences, the Guardian, and TechStars.

→ www.sunnybates.com

"Eventually everything connects—people, ideas, objects. The quality of the connections is the key to quality."

CREATING A KILLER
COLLABORATIVE TEAM

–

David Burkus

In 1995, Kevin Dunbar set up a rather creative
laboratory experiment. He wanted to study how
scientific breakthroughs happened. Dunbar, a
psychologist at McGill University, broke with the
traditional methods of scientific inquiry used in
psychology and opted instead to emulate the field
studies of anthropology and ethnography. Instead
of testing, he would use observation. He set up
cameras inside four prominent microbiology
laboratories in order to study when and how the
scientists' breakthrough insights occurred.[8]

Dunbar's surprising discovery was that most insights didn't actually occur when the researchers were alone in the lab. In fact, the

majority actually occurred during regularly scheduled lab meetings where individual researchers revealed their latest findings and shared their most difficult setbacks with the rest of the team.

In any research laboratory, most experiments are failures or at best yield unexpected results. During these regular meetings, Dunbar observed that the researchers shared their results and also developed analogies trying to describe what might be causing their problem. (Analogies are actually quite common in scientific insight. Consider how Watson and Crick used the twisted ladder analogy to describe the double-helix structure of DNA molecules.)

Dunbar noted that as the researchers developed analogies, and as other researchers built on the ideas around those analogies, the solutions to their problems seemed to simply emerge. Sometimes, a researcher would spend a week vexed by a problem, and the solution would seem to present itself in just ten minutes of discussion with peers. Dunbar also found that the labs with more diverse teams of individuals—people with different areas of expertise who were working on very different types of projects—generated more creative insights and produced more significant research.

But just how diverse did a team need to be for optimal creativity? Dunbar's research didn't answer this question. For that we have to move from the microbiology lab to the Broadway stage.

No Broadway production is created alone. Even so-called "one-man shows" require a crew of people to help with writing, staging, lighting, and everything that goes into taking a production, from the initial idea to opening night. This need for collaboration is what drew the attention of two management professors, Brian Uzzi and Jarrett Spiro. Uzzi and Spiro wanted to know how the creativity and success of a Broadway musical was affected by the level of diversity among collaborators. Many of the artists on Broadway work on more than one musical at a time; as such, they develop relationships between members of their various teams. The two researchers designed a study to examine if the strength or diversity of those relationships affected the success of their work.[9]

Together, Uzzi and Spiro analyzed almost every musical produced on Broadway from 1945 to 1989. The end result was a database of 474 musicals and 2,092 artists, including Broadway legends from Cole Porter to Andrew Lloyd Webber. Once the database was built, the duo analyzed each show to calculate the complex network of collaborations and working relationships between producers, writers, actors, and choreographers. The researchers found that the world of Broadway musicals was indeed a dense and interconnected web, with many individuals working together on a production, then going their separate ways only to find themselves working with some of the same people years later on a new production. This dynamic produced what is now called a "small world network," a fertile ground for teams to connect, collaborate, and disband as needed.

The researchers even found a way to measure the level of repeat collaboration in any given production year, a value they called "small world quotient" or simply Q. The Q score was a measurement of how diverse or homogenous the Broadway production teams from that year were. When Q is high, the teams are densely interconnected; more artists know each other and are working together on multiple projects. When Q is low, there isn't as much familiarity and multiple collaborations are seldom. Uzzi and Spiro then compared each year's

Q score to the level of financial success and critical acclaim achieved by the shows that year.

Given what we know about teams, it would be logical to assume that those production crews with a higher Q—those teams that had lots of experience working together in the past—would perform better and would produce shows that were more creative and successful. Uzzi and Spiro's research found that this assumption held true, but only until a certain point. Instead of a straight line rising in success as it rose in diversity, the trend line looked more like an inverted U. As the Q of a production year went up, representing the diversity of the network structure, so did the year's financial and artistic successes until a certain optimal point, when higher Q actually led to a decrease in the success measurements.

So why did the success start dropping off after a certain point? It turns out that the closeness of a given team affects its performance: Total strangers forced to work together can have problems exchanging ideas, but best friends aren't that good for creativity, either. In the latter case, the collaborators are often so close, and share such a common background, that they end up with the same ideas—a kind of creative groupthink. Ultimately, Uzzi and Spiro found collaborations built from a combination of close connections and fresh perspectives enhance the creative potential of everyone involved. In this scenario, individuals can quickly establish norms for communicating and exchanging ideas, but also benefit from the differing experiences and knowledge brought in by new team members.

Uzzi and Spiro's research also helps to explain the phenomenon in Dunbar's laboratories, where the more diverse teams yielded more creative insights and breakthroughs. If all the scientists had been working on the same experiment and had the same professional backgrounds, they would all think of the same potential explanations. However, in Dunbar's study, the laboratories were running a variety of experiments organized by people from different fields, which meant that everyone benefited from the diverse knowledge of everyone else's past experiences. (It's worth noting that in Dunbar's case, the fact that these were all microbiology labs in particular kept the groups from becoming too diverse).

Taken together, Dunbar's and Uzzi and Spiro's findings imply that the most successful creative projects are generated by teams that include a healthy mix of pre-existing connections, shared experiences, and totally new perspectives. If you're looking to enhance your creative potential, then being on a team helps. But it's not enough to be on any old team. You have to be on a team with the right blend of old and new collaborators.

Do you have a go-to roster of colleagues whom you collaborate with on every project? If so, you might benefit from building a broader network and rotating in collaborators with different perspectives and work experience. Conversely, if you regularly work alone or with a constantly rotating cast of new faces, see if you can introduce an element of stability. Are there one or two colleagues with whom you already have a kind of "creative shorthand"? If so, you might explore integrating them into your projects more regularly to introduce a level of consistency that might be beneficial.

As with anything, finding the right balance is key. Too much familiarity in your creative team can lead to stagnation, while too little can mean you're constantly out of sync and spinning your wheels. The most important takeaway for you as an individual might well lie in understanding the paramount importance of collaboration. If you really want your creative projects to take off, don't go it alone.

DAVID BURKUS is Assistant Professor of Management at the College of Business at Oral Roberts University, where he teaches courses on creativity, innovation, and entrepreneurship. He is the author of The Myths of Creativity: The Truth About How Innovative Companies and People Generate Great Ideas.

→ www.davidburkus.com

"Tell me and I forget, teach me and I remember, involve me and I learn."

— CHINESE PROVERB

LEADING IN A WORLD
OF CO-CREATION

—

Mark McGuinness

Who was the architect of Chartres Cathedral? Don't worry if you don't know the answer. (And *Wikipedia* or Google won't help.) It's a trick question: *there was no architect*. These days, we take it for granted that large buildings are "designed" by a single person, the architect. The actual work of construction is delegated to builders whose job it is to follow the plans and execute the architect's vision.

We don't see Frank Gehry feeding the cement mixer or winching girders into place with a crane. Neither do we see builders designing facades, nor initiating major alterations to a building halfway through a project. But in the Middle Ages, sights like this would have been commonplace.

In his books *The Contractors of Chartres* and *The Master Masons of Chartres*, architect John James argues convincingly that the cathedral was not designed by an architect and then delegated to the builders.[10] In fact, there was no such profession as architect in the modern sense. Instead, the role of architect and chief builder were combined in the person of the Master Builder, who was a skilled craftsman as well as draughtsman.

And just as the Master got his hands dirty with construction, so the other workers on the ground (or up on the scaffold) took responsibility for shaping the big vision. Authority was clearly defined, but the Master's role was not to plan and micromanage everything down to the last pane of glass; instead, he was responsible for shaping the overall vision and coordinating his team's efforts while allowing them freedom to improvise within the overall structure:

> *These buildings were constructed on a far more collective basis than is generally accepted today. . . . The chief builder's job was one of co-ordinating the workforce . . . in a form of activity that was . . . more akin to jazz than to orchestral music.*[11]

Realizing your full creative potential—and that of others—demands the skills of the Master Builder rather than the architect, the jazz impresario rather than the conductor. Not just dreaming up visions, but doing the work of execution; not just solo creation, but co-creation with others; not just issuing commands, but collaborating with expert partners.

LEAD BY EXAMPLE, NOT JUST AUTHORITY

In the Middle Ages, the word "Master" had a very specific meaning: it meant someone who had undergone rigorous formal training in a discipline such as masonry, carpentry, or painting. After an apprenticeship, an aspirant had to produce a "masterpiece"—a piece of work judged good enough to earn the title, authority, and responsibilities of Master and membership in a professional guild.

As Masters rose through the ranks, they did not retire to the corner office or a remote studio. They kept working with their own hands, perfecting their craft and leading by example as well as by authority.

In *Confessions of an Advertising Man*, David Ogilvy wrote that even as the head of a busy agency, he still took time to write occasional advertisements himself, to show his copywriters how it was done. He was following the example of his old boss Monsieur Pitard, head chef of the Hotel Majestic in Paris, who came out of his office once a week and cooked a dish that made it clear who was the best chef in the kitchen.

Keep your "hand in," even if you move into a management role. Doing this will have several benefits: (1) on a personal level, you'll derive satisfaction from doing the work yourself, (2) it will deepen your understanding of the challenges faced by your team, and

(3) since most creatives make judgments based on talent and achievement, you'll maintain the respect of your team.

EVERYTHING IS BUILT ON RELATIONSHIPS

Just as the Cathedral of Chartres is held up by a complex web of stresses and counter-stresses, so the teams who built it were tied together by collaborative relationships—with a similarly delicate balance of stresses. Authority played its part, as well as professional respect and what the builders would have called "fellowship."

If you're working in an agency or studio, you'll be familiar with this atmosphere and the need to build strong relationships with your fellow workers. But even if you're a freelancer or solo artist, your creative production depends on all kinds of people—clients, contractors, suppliers, partners, mentors, assistants, and your professional peers.

So hone your communication skills just as keenly as your craft. Learn to write clear e-mails and compelling copy; to deliver persuasive presentations; to chair a productive meeting; to make those "difficult" conversations go more smoothly. Invest time in networking and building strong working relationships (not the same as friendships). When someone on your team needs help, offer it—what goes around comes around.

IMPROVISE TOGETHER

Unlike modern architects, the cathedral builders did not start with a miniature drawing of the entire building. Instead, they meticulously staked out the dimensions of the building, at full size, on the actual construction site. The details of specific elements—such as the shape of columns, arches, and windows—were worked out as the building progressed by specialist builders who took the lead in different areas.

The basic structure was ordained and measured out by the Master. But at every stage of the work, gaps were left to be filled in by the expertise and ingenuity of individual craftsmen. They paid a lot of attention to detail, because the detail was left to them.

If it sounds incredible that so many interlocking elements of a complex structure could be improvised by workers on the ground, think of *Wikipedia*. The Wikimedia Foundation is responsible for the overall vision and structure of the site. But within this framework, thousands of writers are free to improvise, by writing, editing, and discussing one another's work.

The result is a sprawling yet coherent structure, where articles on the most obscure topics are crafted to the same level of obsessive detail as the gargoyles up on the roof of Chartres, where no one but God and the sculptor's peers would see them.

When you take charge of a project, start by inspiring people with your vision. And make sure all those involved are crystal clear about their responsibilities and non-negotiable deliverables. But don't micro-manage or insist they do everything your way. If you really want to get the best out of them, leave plenty of gaps for them to fill with their creativity and initiative.

BUILD ON OTHERS' WORK

Chartres was not built by a single master but by a succession of nine masters who came and went with the ebb and flow of funding over the years. This meant there was no single comprehensive vision for the cathedral's design—each master built on the work of his predecessor, adapting and altering the design as he saw fit and the work progressed.

One of the unwritten rules of cathedral construction described by James was that whenever a new master started work, he left the previous master's work intact. Instead of razing the stonework and starting afresh, he incorporated its lines and themes in his new construction.

Start to listen to the conversations in your workplace: do people typically build on each other's ideas ("Yes, and …") or block them ("Yes, but") and try to replace them with their own?

How about you? When someone proposes a new idea, is your instinct to accept it and look for ways to develop it, or to critique it and pull it to pieces? When you join a project that others have started, do you look for ways to build on their foundation, or are you tempted to start over from scratch?

From now on, make a conscious effort to build rather than block. Start by asking "What's already working? How can we build on it?" Look for opportunities to praise (sincerely). Say "Yes, and" instead of "Yes, but"—and encourage others to do the same.

(Don't worry, your critical faculty won't disappear. It's too well-built for that.)

WORK FIRST, EGO SECOND

We don't know the names of the Masters of Chartres. According to James, their peers would have recognized their "signature" in the distinctive details of the stonework they produced. This peer recognition—plus their pay and pride in the work—would have been enough.

It was during the Renaissance that visionaries were elevated and put on pedestals, while craftsmen were relegated to the status of hired labor. Artists and designers began to be revered as divine geniuses. Their names became brands, commanding high prices from collectors. They started signing their paintings. We began to learn the names of "architects."

Status, credits, rewards, and awards are all very well. Your professional reputation is important, and there's a time and a place for securing it. But when it's time to start work, put all this out of your mind and focus on the task at hand.

Don't be too proud to listen to others. Ask a lot of questions and pay attention to the answers, not out of politeness but out of respect for their expertise and the knowledge that you can achieve more together than alone. Give them credit and praise for their contributions.

"Co-creation" sounds like a touchy-feely expression, but the reality is that it can be downright scary. Co-creation involves letting go of control, listening—*really listening*—to people around you, and delegating responsibility to them. Most of all, it means building trust: earning the trust of others, trusting them in return, and trusting that together you can build something bigger and more inspiring than any of you could achieve on your own.

MARK MCGUINNESS is a coach for creative professionals. Based in London, he coaches clients all over the world and consults for creative companies. He is the author of the book Resilience: Facing Down Rejection and Criticism on the Road to Success, *and a columnist for 99U.*

→ www.LateralAction.com

KEY
TAKEAWAYS

—

Cultivating Relationships

Get more insights and the desktop wallpaper at:

→ www.99u.com/relationships

· DON'T GO IT ALONE

Seek out fellow travelers—trusted colleagues and collaborators whom you can ask for help, who will tell you the truth, and who will hold you accountable.

· CREATE SOCIAL CONTRACTS

Address what could go wrong in a creative relationship up front. Then, when a conflict does arise, you've created a comfortable space for talking about it.

· TRUST IN GENEROSITY

Focus on how you can help others, and lasting connections will come. The true spirit of networking should be generosity, not obligation.

· ASK AND YE SHALL RECEIVE

Asking always precedes connecting, and if you do it regularly, your network will thrive. Make a weekly habit of reaching out to people whom you admire.

· CROSS-POLLINATION BEGETS CREATIVITY

Try to assemble creative teams that include both veteran collaborators and newbies. Diversity (in the right dosage) accelerates your creative potential.

· ACT LIKE A MASTER BUILDER, NOT A MASTER MIND

Build on—and improvise with—others' ideas and skill sets. If you let everyone shine in his or her area of expertise, your projects will thrive.

CHAPTER FOUR

TAKING

RISKS

–

*How to embrace failure and
take more (and smarter) risks*

Nothing great has ever been achieved by sticking with the status quo. If you want to create something new and different, risk-taking needs to be part of your repertoire.

But that's easier said than done when our brains are hardwired to avoid uncertainty and play it safe. When we think about risks, we think about failure. When we think about failure, we start to get scared. When we start to get scared, our brains send out signals to get the hell out of there.

So how can we overcome our natural tendency to run away from risk? We'll look at the science behind why we fear failure, explore how persistence can create positive outcomes in the face of massive setbacks, and learn how to view our mistakes as valuable data rather than an opportunity to beat ourselves up.

The upside of risk is that—no matter what the outcome—we act, we learn, and we grow. And when tomorrow comes, we're better equipped to face it.

DEMYSTIFYING THE FEAR FACTOR IN FAILURE

—

Michael Schwalbe

On the evening of June 28, 1976, after rehearsing in front of friends for weeks, a twenty-two year-old Jerry Seinfeld walked up onstage at the Catch a Rising Star comedy club in New York City to give his first public performance as a stand-up comic. Seinfeld took the microphone, looked out into audience, and froze. When he finally found his voice, all he could remember were the topics he had prepared to talk about. He rattled them off ("the beach . . . cars . . .") without pausing and then hurried offstage. The entire performance lasted about ninety seconds. As Seinfeld later recounted his first moments in the spotlight, "I couldn't even speak . . . I was so paralyzed in total fear."[12]

Seinfeld's ordeal is not unusual. Researchers are gathering a host of evidence showing that the more we fear failure, the less we succeed.

A recent study led by a team of neuroscientists at Caltech found that when competing in a high-stakes computer game, participants performed worse the more they were concerned about losing.[13]

But science is also revealing that these fears are not only counter-productive, they are overblown. It turns out that humans have a strong tendency to overestimate both the pain of failure and how negatively others perceive our mishaps. To explain why, let's first take a look at why winning the lottery isn't as amazing as you would think.

Imagine that Morpheus from the *Matrix* films offers you a blue pill and a red pill. If you take the blue pill, you wake up having won a two-million-dollar lottery. If you take the red pill, you wake up paralyzed, confined to a wheelchair for the rest of your life. You naturally choose the blue pill and are pleased to find a large sum in your bank account the next morning. You could not think of many things more depressing than being a paraplegic. Some might even think such a life was not worth living. But they would be wrong.[14]

In a famous study on lottery winners and accident victims (including eighteen quadriplegics and eleven paraplegics), within one year of winning the lottery or suffering an accident, something odd occurred. The happiness of lottery winners returned to the same level as the control subjects who did not win any money. Equally surprising, the happiness of accident victims returned to levels above neutral, and a recent study out of Harvard found that paralyzed individuals were no less happy than lottery winners over time.[15] How did this happen?

It's more what *didn't* happen. The high of winning the lottery didn't sustain. Similarly, the despair of becoming a paraplegic didn't stick. Both lottery winners and paraplegics experienced what psychologist Jonathan Haidt calls the adaptation principle.[16] We judge being a lottery winner (or paraplegic) by what it is to *become* one. We often overlook, however, what it is like to actually *be* one.

Humans quickly adapt to new situations. Novelty wears off faster than we expect. When we imagine becoming a lottery winner, we envision only the wondrous things we'd do with our winnings. We don't anticipate the constant harassments of people wanting our money, the complexities of managing it, or the new strains it causes on our social networks and family (so much so that lottery winners actually set up support groups with one another).[17] Nor do we expect, as a quadriplegic, that so much joy could come from things we previously took for granted. As we re-learn even the most basic tasks, we experience progress. And progress feels good.

This is not to say our conditions in life don't matter. Painful changes are unpleasant and our baseline levels of happiness can shift. The key finding is that when we're faced with a small setback or even a massive trauma (such as permanent spinal cord injury), we regularly misjudge the intensity and duration of our emotional reactions. Ultimately, we recover better—and faster—than we expect. Psychologists Daniel Gilbert and Timothy Wilson call this impact bias. Whether it's failing an exam, flunking an interview, or getting fired from a job, their studies have shown that people consistently overestimate the negative impact of such events.[18] And since we expect such failures to be more painful and drawn out than they actually are, we fear them more than we should.

Gilbert and Wilson highlight two phenomena to explain this bias. The first is immune neglect. Just as we have a physical immune system to fight threats to our body, we have a psychological immune system to fight threats to our mental health. We identify silver linings, rationalize our actions, and find meaning in our setbacks. We don't realize how effective this immune system is, however, because it operates largely beneath our conscious awareness.[19] When we think about taking a risk, we rarely consider how good we will be at reframing a disappointing outcome. In short, we underestimate our resilience.

The second reason is focalism. When we contemplate failure from afar, according to Gilbert and Wilson, we tend to overemphasize the focal event (i.e., failure) and overlook all the other episodic details of daily life that help us move on and feel better.[20] The threat of failure is so vivid that it consumes our attention. This happens in part because the areas of the brain we use to perceive the present are the same ones we employ to imagine the future. When we feel afraid of failing at a new business or anxious about the shame of letting investors down and what our peers will think, it's hard to also imagine the pleasure we will get from our next venture and the other everyday activities that are a necessary and enjoyable part of life.

We also overestimate how harshly others will judge us. Researchers Tom Gilovich and Kenneth Savitsky call this the spotlight effect. In their numerous experiments of embarrassing situations—such as flunking an intelligence test or having to wear a Barry Manilow T-shirt in front of colleagues—participants regularly misjudge how negatively others perceive their behavior.[21] We expect others to focus intently on our shortcomings, but we neglect to consider the influence of key peripheral factors, such as people's positive memories of past interactions or how much others are absorbed in their own worlds.

But you may still be wondering, what about the painful sting of regret? According to further research by Gilovich and colleagues, we also miscalculate how long this sting lasts. It hurts at first, but we deal with the pain of regrettable actions better than we think. Our psychological immune system kicks in and helps us make sense of our setback. Failure gives us valuable feedback that we use to address our regrettable actions and improve our situation in the future.

Studies consistently show that when we look back on our lives the most common regrets are not the risks we took, but the ones we didn't. Of the many regrets people describe, regrets of inaction out-number those of action by nearly two to one. Some of the most common include not pursuing more education, not being more assertive, and failing to seize the moment. When people reflect later in life, it is the things they did not do that generate the greatest despair.[22]

We are left with a paradox of inaction. On one hand we instinctively tend to stick with the default, or go with the herd. Researchers call it the status quo bias.[23] We feel safe in our comfort zones, where we can avoid the sting of regret. And yet, at the same time, we regret most those actions and risks we did not take.

Jerry Seinfeld took a few months to recover from his initial deba-cle. He got back up onstage a second time late in the summer of 1976 at the Golden Lion Pub, a seedy bar in Times Square. Again, he was visibly nervous and forgot to segue between jokes, but he barreled through and finished his routine. Jerry continued to perform wherever he could throughout the city, getting increasingly comfortable onstage until he finally landed a paid emcee gig at the newly opened Comic Strip club and became a regular back at Catch a Rising Star.

Five years later, after painstakingly honing his material and reputation, on May 7, 1981, Jerry debuted on *The Tonight Show* with Johnny Carson, followed by years of touring on the road, an eventual HBO special, and finally, in 1989, the pilot for *Seinfeld*, which would go on to earn $2.7 billion from reruns alone and become one of America's all-time favorite television sitcoms.

If Seinfeld hadn't been brave enough to face the audience again after he bombed his first performance, none of that would have happened. Caving to our fears of short-term regret is shortsighted. Ultimately, we serve ourselves better by fearing a failure to act more than fearing failure itself.

MICHAEL SCHWALBE is a PhD candidate in psychology at Stanford University. Previously, Michael worked in investing and research in the finance industry for more than a decade. He has written for 99U and OPEN Forum and consults for companies and NGOs on financial analytics as well as organizational development. Follow him on Twitter @michaelschwalbe.

→ www.michaelschwalbe.com

"Being right keeps you in place, being wrong forces you to explore."

— STEVEN JOHNSON

UNDERSTANDING YOUR ROLE IN RISK

—

John Caddell

The ancient world was a forbidding, frightening place. Humans lived by their wits, surrounded by mortal risks—predators, fires, enemy tribes, floods. No wonder they looked to the gods and invented myths to explain the unknown and protect them from harm. Thousands of years later, human learning and invention has made the world much safer. Yet, we still retain the risk-averse nature of our ancestors.

When we are confronted with situations in which we have to make a decision without all the information we would like to have, we often err on the side of "wait and see," using due diligence as a way to put off risk, or to avoid it completely. What we forget is that even big mistakes can turn out successfully in the end. Embracing risk is really just a function of adopting the right mind-set.

UNDERSTAND THE OPPORTUNITY

When evaluating whether to take a risk, it's easy to see the early-stage pitfalls you could encounter. Imagining the realization of the opportunity is much harder. But not making the attempt guarantees you won't realize the ultimate benefits. It is necessary to broaden the mind, see the bigger picture, and know that with determination obstacles will be overcome.

Former Coca-Cola president Don Keough ran into this trap when his German management team presented a plan to expand into East Germany after the fall of the Berlin Wall in 1989. Believing the budget was too high, Keough vetoed the proposal. Frustrated by Keough's summary rejection, the management team threatened to resign. The head of German operations challenged Keough to look more closely:

"You don't know the potential of East Germany. You've never been there. You rejected it out of hand without considering that this could be a great opportunity. At the very least, you should talk to them again. But I'd like to ask you to do more. Come with me to see East Germany for yourself, first-hand, and make up your own mind." Keough ended up going with his team to East Germany and seeing for himself. After the trip, he said, "My mind was completely changed. We assembled everyone together, and I apologized for being so narrowly focused and so intransigent. Together, we made plans then and there to buy several plants in the east." [24]

Coke's expansion into East Germany was not without missteps. Yet the opportunity was so great, and the team's determination to succeed so strong, they were able to work through the disappointments and setbacks. East Germany became a fast-growing and profitable market for Coke.

ASSERT YOUR AGENCY

We are not powerless in the face of risk. After a decision has been made, we always have the ability to affect our situations to increase the probability of success. This is agency, or the ability to take actions that influence our destiny.

Future Hall of Fame quarterback Peyton Manning found himself without a team when the Indianapolis Colts released him after fourteen seasons. For the first time in his career, Manning had to find a team to play for. He auditioned for San Francisco 49ers, the Arizona Cardinals, and several other teams before signing a three-year contract with the Denver Broncos. Manning said this about his choice:

> *This decision was hard. . . . I had to pick one [team].*
> *I wanted to go to all of 'em at one point. But, like the*
> *other decisions I made in the past, I decided to make*
> *it and not look back. To go from now and make it the*
> *right decision. I have to go to work to make it*
> *the right decision.*

Rather than see his fate as linked to forces outside his control, Manning demonstrates a different view—through hard work, he can make the decision a success. This sense of agency gives him a powerful asset to drive the outcome he wants. If he fails, it will be in spite of his absolute best efforts to succeed.

BE PERSISTENT

"Many of life's failures are people who did not realize how close they were to success when they gave up." So said Thomas Edison. This can be hard to put into practice, however; just ask the producers of the musical *Spider-Man: Turn Off the Dark*.

On February 7, 2011, reviewer Ben Brantley of the *New York Times* wrote this after seeing a preview of the show: "*Spider-Man* is not only the most expensive musical ever to hit Broadway; it may also rank among the worst. . . . [It] is so grievously broken in every respect that it is beyond repair." The scathing review was only one of many calamities to befall the show, including the injuries of several cast members in falls, and a preview in which Spider-Man himself was left hanging helplessly above the audience when his flying harness malfunctioned.

The producers, Jeremiah Harris and Michael Cohl, could have closed the show immediately—standard procedure when a show is universally panned. By contrast, Harris and Cohl showed agency, understanding of opportunity, and persistence in their response to the disasters plaguing the show.

Harris and Cohl shut down *Spider-Man* temporarily. They sought out feedback from audience members and put that feedback to use.

They revised the script. The composers, Bono and the Edge of U2, wrote new lyrics. The producers raised more money (on top of the record $60 million already spent) to revamp the show. *Spider-Man: Turn Off the Dark* re-opened on June 14, 2011.

As the show re-opened, Cohl said this: "The bad news is that it was very expensive, and the good news is that we will not quit and we will make this a success and that's that."

Within a few months, *Spider-Man* was among the highest grossing shows on Broadway and had retained that status a year later. First Lady Michelle Obama and her two daughters had seen the show, as had tens of thousands of others. A long Broadway run, and lucrative touring productions, were assured.

The worst-case scenario in many of the risks we now face is not serious injury or death; it is a financial setback, a blow to the reputation, a ding to the ego. Moreover, the increasing pace and uncertainty of our economic lives increases the cost and risk of, paradoxically, avoiding risk in the first place. Rather than trying to protect ourselves by avoiding decisions, then, wouldn't it be better to embrace the risks we take—and drive the outcome we desire?

JOHN CADDELL curates The Mistake Bank, *which collects stories of business mistakes and failures. He is an executive with more than twenty-five years' experience in information technology product development and sales. John is the author of* The Mistake Bank: How to Succeed by Forgiving Your Mistakes and Embracing Your Failures, *available at Amazon.com.*

→ www.mistakebank.com

"The chief danger in life is that you take too many precautions."

— ALFRED ADLER

Q&A:

RE-ENGINEERING THE WAY WE THINK ABOUT MISTAKES

–

with Tina Seelig

As an entrepreneur, a professor, a neuroscientist, and the executive director of the Stanford Technology Ventures Program, Tina Seelig is uniquely positioned to understand, firsthand, how we think about risk-taking. For more than a decade, Seelig has taught one of Stanford's most popular courses on innovation, in which she engages students in a series of radical creativity exercises that push them to consider surprising problem-solving approaches and to understand their "risk profile." We talked to Seelig about how we can re-engineer our perspectives on risk and why failure is often a precursor to our greatest achievements.

Is there any way to prepare for failure?

People who spend their time on creative endeavors know that failure is a natural part of the creative process and are ready when it happens. As an example, Jeff Hawkins, founder of Palm Computing, Handspring, and Numenta, gets worried when things go too smoothly, knowing that failure must be lurking around the corner. When he was running Handspring, everything was going swimmingly for the release of the original Visor, a new personal digital assistant. But Jeff kept warning his team that something would happen. And it did. Within the first few days of the release of their first product, they shipped about one hundred thousand units. It was remarkable. But the entire billing and shipping system broke down. Some customers didn't receive products they paid for, and others received three or four times as many units as they ordered. This was a disaster, especially for a new business that was trying to build its reputation.

That sounds like a nightmare. What did they do?

The entire team, including Jeff, buckled down and called each and every customer. They asked each person what he or she had ordered, if they had received it, and whether they had been billed correctly. If anything wasn't perfect, the company corrected it on the spot. The key point is that Jeff knew something would go wrong. He wasn't sure what it would be, but he was prepared to deal with anything that came their way. His experience had taught him that failure is inevitable, and that the key to success is not dodging every bullet but being able to recover quickly.

So you think failure is universal? We can't avoid it?

All of our paths are riddled with small and enormous failures. The key is being able to see these experiences as experiments that yield valuable data and to learn what to do differently next time. For most successful people, the bottom is lined with rubber as opposed to concrete. When they face a failure, they hit bottom, sink in, and then bounce back, tapping into the energy of the impact to propel them into another opportunity.

A great example is David Neeleman, the founder of JetBlue. David initially started an airline called Morris Air, which grew and prospered up until he sold it to Southwest Airlines for $130 million. He then became an employee of Southwest. After only five months, David was fired. He was miserable working for them and, as he says, he was driving them crazy. As part of his contract, he had a five-year non-compete agreement that prevented him from starting another airline. That seemed like a lifetime to wait.

After taking time to recover from this blow, David decided to spend that time planning for his next airline venture. He thought through all the details of the company, including the corporate values, the complete customer experience, the type of people they would hire, as well as the details of how they would train and compensate their employees. David says that getting fired and having to wait to start another airline turned out to be the best thing that ever happened to him. When the non-compete period was over, he was ready to hit the ground running. He was able to turn what seemed like a terrible situation into a period of extreme productivity and creativity.

Do you think that certain types of people are better at taking risks than others?

Trying new things requires a willingness to take risks. However, risk-taking is not binary—you aren't a risk taker or not a risk taker. You're likely comfortable taking some types of risks while finding other types uncomfortable. You might not even see the risks that are comfortable for you to take, discounting their riskiness, while you are likely to amplify the risk of things that make you anxious.

For example, you might love flying down a ski slope at lightning speed or jumping out of airplanes, and not even view these activities as risky. Or you might love giving public lectures or taking on daunting intellectual challenges. The first group is drawn to physical risks, the second to social risks, and the third to intellectual risks.

There are five primary types of risks: physical, social, emotional, financial, and intellectual. I often ask people to map their own risk profile. With only a little bit of reflection, each person knows which types of risks he or she is willing to take. They realize pretty quickly that risk-taking isn't uniform.

So how do you start to balance your risk profile? Or should you?

There isn't a need to change your risk profile; however, it is useful to understand it and to pursue the types of risks you feel comfortable taking and to avoid those that make you squirm. This insight allows you to fill out your team with people with complementary risk profiles so that each person plays to his or her strengths, taking on the types of challenges that match their profile. Additionally, asking others to describe their risk profile is a valuable way to get to know what makes them tick and how they can contribute to your organization.

Do you have any strategies for learning how to become more comfortable with failure?

I require all my students to write a failure résumé. That is, to craft a résumé that summarizes all their biggest screw-ups—personal, professional, and academic. For every failure, each student must describe what he or she learned from that experience. Just imagine the looks of surprise this assignment inspires in students who are so used to showcasing their successes. However, after they finish their résumé, they realize that viewing experiences through the lens of failure forced them to come to terms with their mistakes and to view them as a great source of data about what works and what does not.

TINA SEELIG *is the Executive Director of the Stanford Technology Ventures Program as well as a professor in the department of Management Science and Engineering at Stanford University. She teaches courses on creativity and entrepreneurship. Her newest books are* inGenius: A Crash Course on Creativity *and* What I Wish I Knew When I Was 20.

→ Follow her on Twitter at @tseelig

"Enlightened trial and error outperforms the planning of flawless intellects."

— DAVID KELLEY

LEANING INTO UNCERTAINTY

—

Jonathan Fields

Every creative endeavor, from writing a book to designing a brand to launching a company, follows what's known as an Uncertainty Curve. The beginning of a project is defined by maximum freedom, very little constraint, and high levels of uncertainty. Everything is possible; options, paths, ideas, variations, and directions are all on the table. At the same time, nobody knows exactly what the final output or outcome will be. And, at times, even whether it will be. Which is exactly the way it should be.

Over time, the creators or teams begin to act. They spin all the crazy ideas in their heads onto the page, the digital landscape, the canvas, the business. With each trial, they begin to see what's working and what's not. Data and experience begin to replace intuition and leaps of faith. Freedom begins to yield to constraint, the variables and possibilities that created great uncertainty begin to become fact, creating more certainty about what the process will yield and whether it will succeed. The venture and its outcome begin to take form.

Bumps along the way inevitably happen. Ideas that seemed to have great potential bomb, sending the creative team back to the drawing board and ramping them back into higher states of freedom, but also uncertainty.

Finally, through much experimentation, the deed is done. The book is written. The brand is designed. The company is launched. The move made. Freedom, at least with regard to this phase of the endeavor, is gone, consumed by structure and form. Uncertainty has given way to certainty. You now know exactly what it looks and feels like, and whether you were capable of pulling it off.

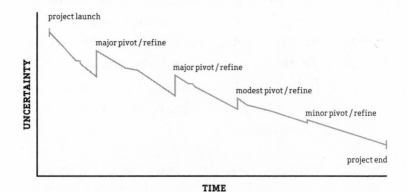

The image on the facing page illustrates this move along the Uncertainty Curve. But, what may not be so apparent is that the speed at which you move along the curve can either kill your ability to create genius or fuel it.

Move too slowly and there's no output. The process becomes consumed by inertia and either suffers from paralysis or moves at a pace that's so slow it all but ensures the endeavor is killed before it ever yields meaningful output. We've all experienced that.

What may be less apparent, though, is that moving too quickly can get you faster to output, but end up yielding something that's far below what you'd have been capable of creating had you stayed in the process longer.

Richard Wiseman actually conducted a fun experiment around this. He assembled two groups of people who identified as either being very lucky or very unlucky. Each was given a newspaper and told to count the number of pictures. The unlucky group took about two minutes. The lucky group took about two seconds. Both came up with the right number. What gives?

Turns out, these were specially printed newspapers. On the inside front cover, above the fold in two-inch block letters, was a message that read: "Stop counting. There are forty-three photographs in this newspaper." The people who identified themselves as unlucky were so focused on the task that they completely ignored the much bigger prize. The people who identified themselves as lucky remained open to the possibility that something outside the rigid instructions might come their way to make the task better or easier.

UNCERTAINTY AS CREATIVE FUEL

A similar thing happens with the creative process. Those who are doggedly attached to the idea they began with may well execute on that idea. And do it well and fast. But along the way, they often miss so many unanticipated possibilities, options, alternatives, and paths that would've taken them away from that linear focus on executing on the vision, and sent them back into a place of creative dissidence and uncertainty, but also very likely yielded something orders of magnitude better.

All creators need to be able to live in the shade of the big questions long enough for truly revolutionary ideas and insights to emerge. They need to stay and act in that place relentlessly through the first, most obvious wave of ideas. Through the second, moving-toward-brutal phase. And then into the revelation phase. But most don't. They give up, backpedal, or settle for good enough when genius lies just around the corner.

Which leaves us with a big question: Why?

Why do people move along the Uncertainty Curve either too slowly or too quickly, killing the project or generating subpar outcomes? Part of the answer may lie in practicalities: team dynamics/dysfunctions or flawed design execution. But a much bigger part of the puzzle lies in what happens in a creator's brain during the process of creation.

Most people are strongly wired to be intolerant of uncertainty. We experience it as pain, fear, anxiety, and doubt. When faced with the need to coexist or, horror of horrors, act in the face of great uncertainty, we recoil. The primal fear center in the brain, the amygdala, lights up, sending chemicals coursing through our bodies that make us physically uneasy, emotionally uncomfortable, and, in short order, spent.

We know the quest to create something from nothing requires us to go to that place. But we're so poorly equipped to handle it, we begin to make decisions based not on what's best for the endeavor, but on what will get us out of that painful place of uncertainty the fastest. For some, that means backing down, becoming stalled or paralyzed. For others, it means rushing to just get it over with. Either way, the end result is either nothing or something far below your true potential.

So how can we live in the shade of uncertainty long enough to birth genius? Three thoughts:

One, simply understanding the psychology of the process allows you to be more mindful of the speed at which you move from freedom to constraint.

Two, when you reframe uncertainty as possibility, the above question changes. Nothing truly innovative, nothing that has advanced art, business, design, or humanity, was ever created in the face of genuine certainty or perfect information. Because the only way to be certain before you begin is if the thing you seek to do has already been done. In which case, you're no longer creating, you're replicating. And that's not why we're here. When you bring the possibility frame to the quest, you'll still feel the butterflies that accompany action in the face of uncertainty, but you'll be better armed to experience them as continuing evidence that what you're working on matters.

Three, there is no universal formula that tells you how quickly to move along the uncertainty curve. It will differ from project to project and be strongly influenced by your unique resources and constraints, both internal and external. What's more important is that you clearly define those resources and constraints, cultivate the mind-set, workflow, environment, and lifestyle needed to fuel action, then act. And elevate learning as a core metric. The enemy of creation is not uncertainty, it's inertia.

JONATHAN FIELDS is a dad, husband, author, speaker, and entrepreneur. His latest book, Uncertainty: Turning Fear and Doubt Into Fuel For Brilliance, *was named the #1 personal development book of 2011 by 800-CEO-READ. Fields blogs at JonathanFields.com, and runs the media and education venture GoodLifeProject.com and book-marketing educational venture TribalAuthor.com.*

→ www.goodlifeproject.com

"Uncertainty is an uncomfortable position.

But certainty is an absurd one."

— VOLTAIRE

MAKING PURPOSEFUL
BETS IN A RANDOM WORLD

—

Frans Johansson

At some point in the summer of 1907, Picasso completed what was to become one of the most important paintings of his career, *Les Demoiselles d'Avignon*. Its style was such a departure from the paintings before it, and it had such a provocative theme—five prostitutes staring at the viewer—that the painting simply demanded attention. It has since gone down in history as a cornerstone in modernism.

On December 10, 2009, Rovio released the iPhone version of its game Angry Birds. After topping the charts in a few European countries it quickly hit the United States with full force and changed the world of casual games. Within two years it had been downloaded almost a billion times, and it is now one of the most played games in history.

In March 2008, a young woman named Bethenny Frankel joined the cast of a new reality show called *The Real Housewives of New York City*. The exposure allowed her to highlight a new product of hers, Skinnygirl Margarita. It soon took off and became a sensation among women looking for a low-calorie night out. She later sold the brand for $64 million.

Now, what do Picasso, Rovio, and Frankel all have in common? On the face of it, seemingly nothing. But dig a little bit deeper and you will find one of the most fundamental truths about success in design, business, and innovation generally. It comes down to this: none of these people or organizations really had much of a clue as to exactly *which one* of their ideas was going to work. In fact, the success garnered in each of these examples is the result of harnessing unexpected insights and placing bets all with an unknown outcome. In other words, success is more serendipitous and random than we think.

This may seem quite surprising. We are used to thinking that successful people and companies have cracked some secret code, and when we retell the stories of how they did it we do so in order to understand how we can do the same. Take Rovio, for instance. The Finnish company behind Angry Birds was able to not only design an amazing game, but also to develop a killer marketing strategy for it. Instead of focusing on the massive US market first, they focused on smaller European markets such as Greece and the Czech Republic. Those markets had relatively few downloads, and Rovio figured it would be pretty easy to reach the top spot on those lists, which they were able to do. With those wins in hand they turned to the United Kingdom, where the game hit the number one spot virtually overnight. After that, they decided they finally had enough momentum to go for the US market.

Everything about this story suggests that Rovio has not only a firm grasp on winning game design, but also on how to market games successfully. But if they had all that, why did they wait eight years to use it? Because that was how long they had been around before releasing Angry Birds. It was their fifty-second game. None of the games that came before it had even a fraction of Angry Bird's success. Instead, this one game brought the company back from the brink and has allowed it to build a franchise that may last years. Soon after Angry Bird's success, Rovio was valued at $1 billion.

Success, it turns out, has far less to do with figuring out exactly what the right next move is and far more to do with serendipity and randomness. A rare few of us operate in a world where the rules never or rarely change, such as chess or tennis or golf, and in such a world you can practice your way to domination. Hard, consistent work brings you glory, since you know exactly what you have to do—you just have to do it better than everyone else, often after having put more than ten thousand hours or so of hard work behind it. This so-called ten-thousand-hour rule, popularized by Malcolm Gladwell, does not apply in any other endeavor, however. Neither Reed Hastings nor Richard Branson had ten thousand hours of practice when they became leaders in their various fields.

Not only that, we frequently see people and organizations we consider brilliant follow up great success with mediocre or uninspiring fare. Phenomenal CEOs disappoint, kick-ass movie directors leave us frustrated, and successful entrepreneurs fail to live up to their investors' expectations. And sometimes they can go from a success to a failure without any real rhyme or reason. Filmmaker Woody Allen is a prime example of this throughout his career. But so is virtually every single innovator. Evan Williams, one of the co-founders of Twitter, first created Blogger, which was a great success. He then created Odeo, a podcasting company that did not really work out all that well. But he followed *that* up with Twitter. This all suggests that success is far more random and serendipitous than most of us would like to acknowledge. So a question immediately follows: Given that, what should you do about it?

PLACE MANY BETS

If it is difficult to predict just what exactly is going to be successful, it follows that you have to keep trying. The more times you try, the more likely that you will create successful designs, start-ups, or pieces of art. If we look at the most successful innovators throughout history, we find that they have all been stunningly productive. They keep trying over and over again. Pablo Picasso created somewhere between fifty thousand and one hundred thousand works of art in his lifetime. He did not have the ability to simply decide that any given piece of art was going to become a masterpiece, such as *Les Demoiselles d'Avignon*. Instead, he set himself up for great success by rolling the dice over and over. Many of his canvases have collected dust in cellars around the world, and with good reason. They sucked. Picasso could not predict with any certainty which of his pieces would become celebrated and which would be recycled. He was, in essence, placing a bet that a percentage of his work would take hold. It therefore follows that Picasso's output gave him an incredible edge in becoming successful.

The same is true for Bethenny Frankel. What many people don't realize is that her appearance on Bravo's reality show was part of a long list of bets she made for success. She never knew which bet was going to work (although she most likely believed all of them would succeed at their inception), but she attempted nearly everything and anything. First she started a party-planning company, then a pashmina-import business, and followed it up with an unsuccessful health food store. Next, she launched a health-conscious bakery and then applied for Donald Trump's hit show *The Apprentice* but was not selected. Soon after that, she landed a part on Martha Stewart's ill-fated *The Apprentice: Martha Stewart* and went on to launch a custom-meals business. She wrote a column for *Health* magazine, which led to an endorsement deal with Pepperidge Farm. After eight bets she joined the cast of Bravo's new reality show, *The Real Housewives of New York City*, where she was able to launch Skinnygirl, a cocktail mix that she then sold for $64 million. In other words, she gave herself many chances to be successful. In an increasingly unpredictable world, you have to leverage the statistical advantage of randomness by placing many bets.

MAKE THE BETS SMALL

If you should place many bets to increase your chances of success, then it also follows that you cannot afford to do so if those bets are large. If just one of those large bets fails, you may not get a second chance, since you will be out of resources. Unfortunately, we tend to believe that if we just had *more* money or *more* resources we could increase our chances of success. The facts on the ground don't support such a view.

For instance, Apple spent $500 million developing a handheld computing device, the Newton, during the late eighties and early nineties. It was a complete failure. Meanwhile, Palm Computing spent $3 million developing the PalmPilot, the fastest selling computer product in the nineties. More money did not make the difference. What did? Well, the Pilot was actually Palm's second attempt at getting it right. They had spent only $4 million creating a truly awful device called the Zoomer, which allowed them enough money to try again. Apple, on the other hand, only tried once.

By limiting the resources behind bets, by placing what entrepreneur Peter Sims calls "little bets," we can place more of them. When Yngve Bergqvist created the Ice Hotel, in the town of Jukkasjärvi in northern Sweden, it stunned people across the world. The entire hotel is made of ice—walls, ceiling, beds, tables, everything. Most of us would have considered such an idea close to impossible to come up with, and if we had thought of it, we would discard it as crazy. But Bergqvist never started with the Ice Hotel in mind. Instead, he came up with many smaller ideas that, step by step, led to the Ice Hotel.

First, he created a small ice exhibit by flying a group of ice sculptures over from Japan. It gained some unexpected interest. The next winter he created a building made out of snow with an art gallery exhibit inside. The year after that he created a building made out of ice that had interesting exhibits inside, such as an ice bar and a movie screen made out snow. It was at that point that a team of backpackers approached Bergqvist asking to sleep on a bed made out of ice and said they were willing to pay for it. Who could have guessed it? The winter that followed marked the first time Bergqvist actually created the Ice Hotel—a direct result of his having the resources to try something over and over again.

The world is random and unpredictable, which means that it is close to impossible to outline exactly what your next best move is. But you *can* explore it—by doing and trying. Just make sure you don't go all in before you've figured out that it works.

FRANS JOHANSSON *lives in Brooklyn and is the author of* The Click Moment *and the international bestseller* The Medici Effect. *He is the founder of the global innovation strategy firm the Medici Group, which works with corporations, NGOs, and governments around the world to break new ground in an uncertain world.*

→ www.themedicigroup.com

KEY
TAKEAWAYS
—

Taking Risks

Get more insights and the desktop wallpaper at:
→ www.99u.com/risk-taking

• APPRECIATE YOUR ADAPTABILITY

Be aware that when you fail, you will adapt to the new situation much more quickly than you expect. Setbacks often have a silver lining.

• TAKE ACTION TO AVOID REGRET

Fear a failure to act more than you fear failure itself. Most people's biggest regrets are the opportunities they did not act on, not those they did.

• DON'T GO ALL IN

Try to make small bets for the initial test-runs of your project or idea. It's hard to predict what will take off, and this limits your exposure to risk.

• MISTAKES ARE INFORMATION

Mine your "failures" for valuable data about what works and what doesn't. As long as you learn from the process, it's not a mistake.

• DIVE INTO UNCERTAINTY

Don't be afraid to live in the shade of big questions. Uncertainty and ambiguity are a necessary part of risk-taking and the creative process.

• ACCEPT YOUR AGENCY

Embrace your power to make the outcome of any risk a success. Almost any situation can be turned around with persistence and ingenuity.

A FINAL

REFLECTION

—

*A parting message on the challenge
(and the possibility) of potential*

THE BETTER YOU

—

Jack Cheng

Someone is sitting at your desk. There is something familiar about this person. From a distance, this person bears a striking resemblance to you: they have the same frame, the same face, the same features as you. But as you get closer, you begin to notice subtle differences between this person and yourself. They look like they eat healthier and exercise a little more regularly. Their posture is slightly better and their clothes have fewer wrinkles. This person is the Better You.

The Better You knows the same things you know. They've had the same successes you've had, and they've made the same mistakes.

They strive for the same virtues and falter to the same vices. The Better You procrastinates, too. The Better You is not perfect. But the difference between you and the Better You is that the latter reacts a little faster, with a little more willpower. They practice their virtues a little more often and succumb to their vices a little less often. They rein in their procrastination a little quicker. They start their work a little earlier. They know when to take a break a little sooner.

The Better You knows, just as you know, that doing what you love is difficult but worthwhile. They know, just as you know, that the difficulty is what makes it worthwhile in the first place. They know, as you know, that if everything was easy, nothing would have significance, and you wouldn't need to adopt new metaphors or read new books about how to do the work you should be doing.

The Better You is your believable possible. Your believable possible is your potential in any given moment, the person you know at your very core that you are capable of being at this instant. Your believable possible exists at the edge of your perceived ability. Your believable possible is frightening and uncomfortable, but not to the point of paralysis. Your believable possible is just uncomfortable enough. We all have different believable possibles. Bruce Lee's believable possible was being the most dangerous man in the world. Muhammad Ali's was being the greatest boxer of all time. Your own believable possible may be slightly less ambitious. But only you know what your own believable possible is.

The Better You is not a fixed, singular being. The Better You springs new from each moment, is born and dies with each action you take. Each action creates a new set of possibilities. The Better You is an alternate dynamic present, rather than a fixed, static past.

Measuring yourself against the Better You is no mere matter of racing to beat the person you were the day before. Instead, you're racing to keep up with the person you could be right now.

The Better You wants you to meet them where they are. The Better You is the ant that has strayed from the colony and discovered a source of food. The Better You knows the way. It says: *follow me*. And even when there is no food in sight, you know where the trail will take you in the end. The Better You will never lead you astray. So you follow the trail. You sit at the desk and place your hands on your tools—on your keyboard and mouse, your notebook and pen, your palette and brush—and you start on your way.

There are the rare moments of alignment, moments when you reunite with the Better You, when you match the Better You move for move. They are sitting at the desk and working and writing and sketching, and you are sitting at the same desk and working and writing and sketching. You and the Better You are occupying the same physical space and the same mental space. You are completely engaged in the work before you. And when you are doing the work you should be doing, the work the Better You is doing, you become whole, fully *there*.

The joy of alignment makes alignment more frequent, and as alignment becomes more frequent, something interesting happens: you begin to see a different person, a *better* Better You. The new Better You is slightly out of reach, just as the old one was, because there is no limit to Better. Better is the mechanized rabbit on the rail at a greyhound race. Better is propelled by motors and microprocessors and magic and things our dog-brains cannot comprehend, our dog-bodies cannot outrun.

But the Better You knows, just as you know, that the thrill is in the chase, that happiness is motion, and that fulfillment is the constant striving for that which is just beyond our reach. The Better You knows this is the way it has always been, and the way it always will be. And you know it, too.

JACK CHENG is a writer, designer, and entrepreneur based in Brooklyn. He is the author of These Days, *a novel about the human side of technology, published in spring 2013.*

→ www.jackcheng.com

"Decide that you want it more than you are afraid of it."

— BILL COSBY

ACKNOWLEDGMENTS

—

My heartiest thanks must go to our absolutely incredible brain trust of contributors: Teresa Amabile, Sunny Bates, Scott Belsky, Ela Ben-Ur, Michael Bungay Stanier, David Burkus, John Caddell, Ben Casnocha, Jack Cheng, Jonathan Fields, Joshua Foer, Heidi Grant Halvorson, Frans Johansson, Steven Kramer, Steffen Landauer, Mark McGuinness, Cal Newport, Bob Safian, Michael Schwalbe, Tony Schwartz, Tina Seelig, and Scott H. Young. This book would not exist without your insights and expertise. Thank you so much for your time, energy, and generosity.

I owe many thanks for the beautiful cover design and interior layout of this book to the vision of Behance co-founder and chief of design Matias Corea—one of my absolute favorite creative collaborators— and to the excellent eye of our talented designer Raewyn Brandon.

I am also indebted to Katie Salisbury for her enthusiasm and editorial guidance, to Courtney Dodson for shepherding this book gracefully through production, to 99U managing editor Sean Blanda for great feedback on drafts, and to the entire Behance and Amazon teams for their incredible support, talent, and tenacity.

Last, I must extend much, much appreciation to Scott Belsky for his invaluable input on shaping this book series, and—more important— for believing in me. Having the chance to lead 99U as part of Behance's mission to empower the creative world has been—and will continue to be—an incredible and invigorating opportunity for which I am deeply grateful.

— *JOCELYN K. GLEI, editor-in-chief, 99U*

ABOUT 99U

—

99U is Behance's effort to deliver the "missing curriculum" that you didn't get in school, highlighting best practices for making ideas happen. We do this through interviews, articles, and videos on our Webby Award–winning website at 99u.com, our annual 99U Conference in New York City, our bestselling book *Making Ideas Happen*, and our ongoing 99U book series, which includes *Manage Your Day-to-Day* and this book, *Maximize Your Potential*.

→ *www.99u.com*

ABOUT THE EDITOR

—

As editor-in-chief and director, Jocelyn K. Glei leads the 99U in its mission to provide the "missing curriculum" on making ideas happen. She oversees the 99u.com website—which has won two Webby Awards for Best Cultural Blog—and leads the curation and execution of the popular 99U Conference, which has presented talks from visionary creatives including Jack Dorsey, Beth Comstock, John Maeda, Jonathan Adler, Stefan Sagmeister, Jad Abumrad, and many more. She is also the editor of the 99U book series, which includes *Manage Your Day-to-Day* and this book, *Maximize Your Potential.*

Prior to joining Behance and 99U, Jocelyn was the global managing editor at the online media company Flavorpill, leading development of new editorial products. She has also consulted with dozens of brands and agencies, from Herman Miller to PSFK to Huge Inc, on content strategy and web launches. She is passionate about creating content-driven products that people love.

→ *www.jkglei.com*

ENDNOTES
—

1. Kevin Kelly, "Techno Life Skills," *The Technium*, April 28, 2009. http://www.kk.org/
    thetechnium/archives/2011/04/techno_life_ski.php.

2. Thomas Friedman, "The Start-Up of You," *New York Times*, July 12, 2011.

3. Tina Seelig, *What I Wish I Knew When I Was 20* (New York: HarperOne, 2009) 122.

4. Mueller, C. M. and Dweck, C. S. "Praise for Intelligence Can Undermine Children's
    Motivation and Performance." *Journal of Personality and Social Psychology* 75, no.
    1 (1998): 33-52.

5. Baumeister, Roy F.; Bratslavsky, Ellen; Muraven, Mark; Tice, Dianne M. "Ego
    Depletion: Is the Active Self a Limited Resource?" *Journal of Personality and Social
    Psychology* 74, no. 5 (May 1998): 1252–1265.

6. Phillippa Lally, Cornelia H. M. van Jaarsveld, Henry W. W. Potts, Jane Wardle. "How
    Are Habits Formed: Modelling Habit Formation in the Real World." *European
    Journal of Social Psychology* 40, no. 6 (Oct 2010): 998–1109.

7. Ivan P. Pavlov, "Conditioned Reflexes: An Investigation of the Physiological
    Activity of the Cerebral Cortex," *Classics in the History of Psychology*, accessed
    March 4, 2013, http://psychclassics.yorku.ca/Pavlov.

8. Kevin Dunbar, "How Scientists Really Reason: Scientific Reasoning in Real-World
    Laboratories," in *Mechanisms of Insight*, edited by Robert J. Sternberg and Janet
    Davidson (Cambridge, MA: MIT Press, 1995), 365–395.

9. Brian Uzzi and Jarrett Spiro, "Collaboration and Creativity: The Small World Problem," *American Journal of Sociology* 111, no. 2 (2005): 447–504.

10. John James, *The Contractors of Chartres.* 2 volumes. (Wyong, Australia: West Grinstead Publishing, 1979–81); John James, *The Master Masons of Chartres* (London, New York, Chartres, and Sydney: West Grinstead Publications, 1990).

11. Roger Coleman, *The Art of Work* (London: Pluto Press, 1988) 15.

12. Jerry Oppenheimer, *Seinfeld: The Making of American Icon* (New York: HarperCollins Publishers, 2002), 116–120; Kathleen Tracy, *Jerry Seinfeld: The Entire Domain* (Toronto: Carol Publishing, 1998) 19–20.

13. V. S. Chib et al., "Neural Mechanisms Underlying Paradoxical Performance for Monetary Incentives Are Driven by Loss Aversion," *Neuron* 74, no. 3 (May 2012): 582–594.

14. K. Gerhart, J. Koziol-McLain, S.R. Lowenstein, G.G. Whiteneck, "Quality of Life Following Spinal Cord Injury: Knowledge and Attitudes of Emergency Care Providers," *Annals of Emergency Medicine* 23 no. 4 (May 1994): 807–812.

15. P. Brichman, D. Coates, and R. Janoff-Bulman, "Lottery Winners and Accident Victims: Is Happiness Relative?" *Journal of Personality and Social Psychology* 36 no. 8 (1978): 917–927; H. Hayward, *Lottery Winners and Accident Survivors: Happiness Is Relative.* Poster presented at the fourteenth annual meeting of the Society for Personality and Social Psychology, New Orleans (2013).

16. Jonathan Haidt, *The Happiness Hypothesis* (New York: Basic Books, 2006) 82–86.

17. H. R. Kaplan, *Lottery Winners: How They Won and How Winning Changed Their Lives* (New York: Harper and Row, 1978).

18. T. D. Wilson and D. T. Gilbert, "Affective Forecasting," *Advances in Experimental Social Psychology 35* (2003): 345–411.

19. D. T. Gilbert et al., "Immune Neglect: A Source of Durability Bias in Affective Forecasting," *Journal of Personality and Social Psychology* 75, no. 3 (1998): 617–638.

20. T. D. Wilson et al., "Focalism: A Source of Durability Bias in Affective Forecasting," *Journal of Personality and Social Psychology* 78, no. 5 (2000): 821–836.

21. K. Savitsky, N. Epley, and T. Gilovich, "Do Others Judge Us as Harshly as We Think? Overestimating the Impact of Our failures, Shortcomings, and Mishaps," *Journal of Personality and Social Psychology* 81, no. 1 (Jul 2001): 44–56; T. Gilovich, V. H. Medvec, and K. Savitsky, "The Spotlight Effect in Social Judgment: An Egocentric Bias in Estimates of the Salience of One's Own Actions and Appearance," *Journal of Personality and Social Psychology* 78, no. 2 (Feb 2000): 211–222.

22. N. J. Roese and A. T. Summerville, "What We Regret Most... and Why," *Personality and Social Psychology Bulletin* 31, no. 9 (Sep 2005): 1273–1285; T. Gilovich, V. H. Medvec, and D. Kahneman, "Varieties of Regret: A Debate and Partial Resolution," *Psychological Review* 105, no. 3 (1998): 602–605; T. Gilovich and V. H. Medvec, "The Experience of Regret: What, When, and Why," *Psychological Review* 102, no. 2 (1995): 379–395.

23. W. Samuelson and R. Zeckhauser, "Status Quo Bias in Decision Making," *Journal of Risk and Uncertainty* 1 (1988): 7–59.

24. Donald R. Keough, "The Ten Commandments of Business Failure," *Portfolio* (2008): 63-64.

INDEX

_